The
NEW VAMPIRE'S
HANDBOOK

EDITED AND WITH AN INTRODUCTION BY
THE VAMPIRE MILES PROCTOR

The
NEW VAMPIRE'S
HANDBOOK

A GUIDE FOR CREATURES OF THE NIGHT

WRITTEN BY
JOE GARDEN, JANET GINSBURG, CHRIS PAULS,
ANITA SERWACKI, AND SCOTT SHERMAN

SQUARE PEG

Published by Square Peg

2 4 6 8 10 9 7 5 3 1

Copyright © Joe Garden, Janet Ginsburg, Chris Pauls,
Anita Serwacki and Scott Sherman 2009

The authors have asserted their right under the Copyright, Designs
and Patents Act 1988 to be identified as the authors of this work

This book is sold subject to the condition that it shall not,
by way of trade or otherwise, be lent, resold, hired out,
or otherwise circulated without the publisher's prior
consent in any form of binding or cover other than that
in which it is published and without a similar condition,
including this condition, being imposed on the subsequent purchaser

First published in Great Britain in 2009 by
Square Peg
Random House, 20 Vauxhall Bridge Road,
London SW1V 2SA

www.rbooks.co.uk

Addresses for companies within The Random House Group Limited can be found at:
www.randomhouse.co.uk/offices.htm

The Random House Group Limited Reg. No. 954009

A CIP catalogue record for this book
is available from the British Library

ISBN 9780224086462 (hardback)
ISBN 9780224086479 (trade paperback)

The Random House Group Limited supports The Forest Stewardship Council (FSC),
the leading international forest certification organisation. All our titles that are printed on
Greenpeace approved FSC certified paper carry the FSC logo. Our paper procurement policy
can be found at www.rbooks.co.uk/environment

Mixed Sources
Product group from well-managed
forests and other controlled sources
www.fsc.org Cert no. TT-COC-2139
© 1996 Forest Stewardship Council
FSC

Printed and bound in Great Britain by Clays Ltd, St Ives Plc

FOR ZLATAN

Contents

INTRODUCTION ... ix

HEALTH AND WELFARE

1. YOUR NEW BODY ... 3
2. YOUR NEW POWERS ... 9
3. WEAKNESSES ... 16
4. MORTAL ENEMIES ... 27
5. TIME ... 35
6. EXISTENTIAL CRISES ... 39
7. VAMPIROSEXUALITY ... 43
8. FANGS AND ORAL HYGIENE ... 47

FEEDING

9. NOURISHMENT ... 55
10. SELECTING AND LURING PREY ... 60
11. FIVE STEPS FOR A SUCCESSFUL FEEDING ... 67
12. ANIMALTARIANISM ... 71
13. DISASTER PREPAREDNESS ... 74
14. ALLUDING TO YOUR IDENTITY FOR AMUSEMENT AND FRIVOLITY ... 79

VAMPIRE-HUMAN RELATIONS

15. A SPECIAL NOTE REGARDING HUMANS ... 85
16. VAMPIRE-HUMAN LOVE ... 86
17. VAMPIRE FANATICS ... 91

18. WHAT TO DO IF YOU SEE A HUMAN YOU KNEW DECADES AGO	97
19. FAKING YOUR WAY THROUGH A MEAL	99
20. AVOIDING THE MEDIA	104
21. GETTING IN: INVITE-ONLY BUILDINGS	109

SOCIETY AND CULTURE

22. FINDING AND APPROACHING OTHER VAMPIRES	117
23. COVENS	121
24. FEUDS	128
25. VAMPIRE DIVERSITY	134
26. SOCIAL RESPONSIBILITY	137
27. RELOCATING	140
28. SLAVES	143
29. FAMILIARS	148

LIFESTYLE

30. KEEPING UP WITH THE TIMES	153
31. STYLE	158
32. ACTING YOUR AGE	163
33. SCRAPBOOKING	167
34. FINANCES	170
35. COFFINS	175
36. TRAVEL	178
37. IS MENTORING FOR YOU?	184

APPENDICES

APPENDIX I: THE RULING FAMILIES	191
APPENDIX II: GLYPH GUIDE	195
APPENDIX III: TEMPORARY LAIRS	197
APPENDIX IV: ONLINE RESOURCES	201
GLOSSARY	207
AFTERWORD	211
ACKNOWLEDGMENTS	213

Introduction

IF YOU ARE READING THIS, you are a vampire.

There were countless other books in the store, yet you arrived at this one. Drawn to its warm glow, lured by the faint whiff of blood mixed in with the ink, you were brought to this handbook by your new vampiric senses. If you keep reading, you will find that these senses are good for a great deal more than book browsing. In fact, a whole new world of near-unlimited power is on the dark horizon. This guide will show you that world.

As you've realized by now, being turned into a vampire is the easy part. Actually *becoming* a vampire is far more difficult.

Unfortunately, many of the newly turned are saddled with lazy or contemptuous mentors, and instead of receiving knowledge passed down from sage master to eager apprentice, many of our kind find themselves alone. Some have been abandoned by thrill-seeking vampiric procreators who slink off after the instant gratification of turning another ends and they are confronted by the burden of guiding a new creature of the night. Others remain perpetual neophytes because they had the misfortune of being turned by another novice with no advice to offer.

If you find yourself in such wretched circumstances, do not despair. I am here to help. My friend, this is a book you truly cannot live forever without.

But who am I? Why am I worthy of providing this guidance? You are right to ask. Allow me to tell you about myself.

I was born Milos Prockofijev. In the year 1542 I was a tailor and clothier in Pozsony, a town at the foot of the Carpathian Mountains in what is now Bratislava, Slovakia. It was a dark time in my country. The Turks had just overrun the Kingdom of Hungary and our region was flooded with Turkish handicrafts. The workmanship was not all that impressive, but nonetheless they became all the rage and none of the foreign invaders wanted a local hand-tailoring their garments. Suddenly it was "*çatma*-this" and "*kemha*-that" and soon poor Prockofijev couldn't even give away his fine Pozsonian goods. My livelihood was slowly draining away. That was, until the evening Zlatan entered my shop.

Zlatan was a striking, mysterious gentleman, and by the passementerie detailing and golden braids on the flap of his *mente*, I could tell he was a man of extraordinary wealth. He strolled about the floor, delicately handling my fabrics, before turning to me with a broad, tight-lipped smile.

"You are a fine craftsman, and I admire your work," he said. "How would you like to leave your life here and become my exclusive tailor? I'm looking for someone . . . long-term." I contemplated his offer. Zlatan had an impressive frame, and I imagined the many refined creations I could stitch for him. Pozsony no longer held anything for me, so I agreed to accompany him into the night.

Zlatan led me to his villa and asked that I fit him for an evening cloak. As I was sizing his neck, he unexpectedly placed his hand to my wrist and asked for my measuring tape. I complied, and curiously, he began measuring my neck. "Before we proceed," he whispered, "I have something to give you that I believe will be a perfect fit."

Zlatan opened his mouth, and in an instant a pair of daggerlike fangs extended past his lips and plunged into my neck. With that, I donned the immortal coil.

No longer was I the tailor Milos Prockofijev. I became the Vampire Milos Prockofijev.

A new vampire has many questions. I was no different but had a fine teacher in Zlatan. At night he taught me how to seduce, how to feed, how to move at astonishing speeds without tearing my pants. The next few centuries were wonderful. Zlatan and I feasted on the whole of Europe and beyond.

And then in 1897, the novel *Dracula* was released.

Suddenly, things changed. Mortals in urban areas who were previously oblivious to our activities began to obsess about ageless beings with terrifying fangs who walked in the night. There wasn't a tavern we could enter that didn't immediately fill with whispers. Several times Zlatan and I were even chased by mobs too large for us to kill.

Over the next decade, public awareness of vampires in Europe rose to dangerous levels and I thought it a perfect time to explore the fresh culling grounds of America. Zlatan, though, would not join me. His attachment to the Old World was too strong. He gave his blessing for me to leave his stewardship but made me promise to share my knowledge with the American vampires I created, as he had shared his with me. Before leaving, I wove him an ornate black tapestry to commemorate our time together.

I arrived on Ellis Island on April 17, 1907, where my name was changed from Milos Prockofijev to Miles Proctor. Perhaps a little banal, but it certainly aided in my assimilation. In America, I discovered many new enthusiasms: capitalism, automobiles, the Charleston. However, there was one discovery I did not enjoy making, and that was the sheer number of vampires who had been turned so poorly, with so little guidance, that they had virtually no idea how to thrive.

I met Frankie, a vampire turned in Virginia at the dawn of the Civil War, who still did not know with certainty if a crucifix could harm him. I met Celeste, an exquisite vampire turned only years before by an egocentric theater understudy too preoccupied with his career to answer even the most basic of her questions. I met Bill Jackson, a 115-year-old machinist from Pennsylvania, who erroneously believed it was possible for a vampire to stand on the ceiling. And I have met thousands more like them since.

Many of their queries were practical: What can I feed on? What can hurt me? How do I stay financially solvent? Others were more personal: Am I capable of love? Am I still a sexual being in the human sense? Should I feel remorse? All lessons I had learned within my first fifty years with Zlatan.

For decades, these lost immortals had begged their so-called mentors for knowledge, to little or no avail. Through no fault of their own, their ineptitude had often landed them in dangerous situations. I did my best to give them pointers, but one vampire can take on only so many subjects.

I knew then what I had to do. I took it upon myself to write this book—the book you are now holding in your cold, undead hands. After just over seventy-five years of writing, rewriting, and fact-checking, it is done.

Make no mistake, the tome you hold has power—and so do you. It is time for you to take charge of that power and begin to wield it.

It does not matter who you were as a human. It does not matter if you look old or young. It does not matter if you came to the fold willingly or not. If you are holding this book, from this night forward, you can face eternity with confidence.

I am giving you nearly five hundred years of firsthand insight and experience. Use it to assuage your fears and concerns. Use it to become the spectacular creature you most certainly are.

This is the tapestry I have woven for you, my friend.

Welcome to the night.

—THE VAMPIRE MILES PROCTOR,
NÉ MILOS PROCKOFIJEV

HEALTH AND WELFARE

1

YOUR NEW BODY

FROM THE MOMENT you first ran your tongue along your teeth after the transformation, it was clear that your body had undergone changes. But to what extent? It isn't just the fangs that are new. Many functions of your former body have dramatically increased, slowed, or stopped altogether. Each modification occurs so you can become a sleeker, more effective blood-obtaining-and-processing machine. Below are the most dramatic improvements.

DIGESTIVE-CIRCULATORY SYSTEM

The nutritional and dietary needs of your body have changed. You now eat from only one food group, blood, which, when consumed, is absorbed through arteries of the stomach wall (1) and small intestine (2). Because of this, your stomach no longer produces acid, and your saliva no longer contains enzymes to break down starches. Instead, your saliva contains new enzymes that prevent the blood from coagulating. Any blood that is not absorbed by the stomach or

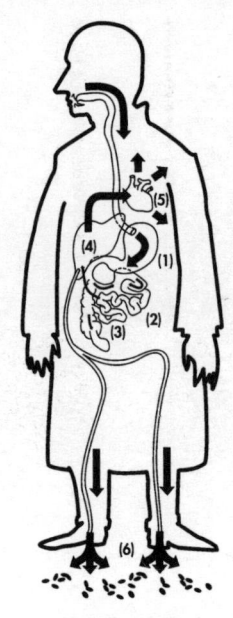

The digestive-circulatory and excretory systems

small intestine makes its way to the newly enlarged appendix (3), where it is stored.* The imbibed blood is whisked to the liver (4), where impurities are filtered out. From there, the **purified blood** passes through your heart (5), which sends it to the rest of your body. The blood's vitality is then slowly absorbed through a biochemical process that releases light-negating **hemo-photon particles,** invisible to the naked eye.

EXCRETORY/URINARY SYSTEM

A vampire's body utilizes 98.9 percent of the blood it processes, so there is far less waste to remove. Consequently, your bladder and

---

*Though humans who have had their appendices removed can and do become vampires, they need to feed far more often.

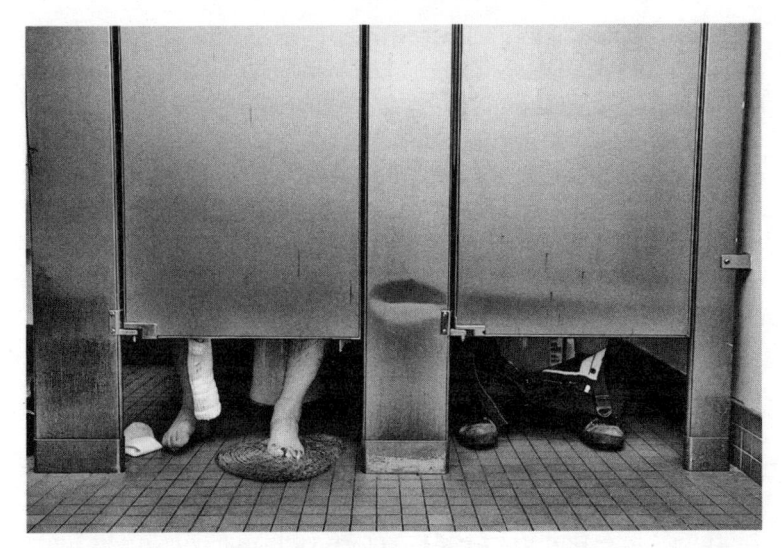

A well-prepared vampire should always have two changes of socks readily available.

large intestine are no longer necessary, and effectively shut down. The kidneys likewise shrink, and your ability to generate the blood-production hormone erythropoietin also halts. The little waste left to remove—dead blood-cell walls and chemical impurities—is discreetly flushed from the body via the sweat ducts (6) of the feet.

INTEGUMENTARY SYSTEM

Undead is not dead. Hair and nails continue to grow, albeit stronger and more slowly.* Your new nails, if grown long, can be used effectively as gouging or slashing implements. A vampire's skin will continue to grow as well, but instead of flaking off, the base components

---

*An old saw maintains that human hair and fingernails grow after death. This is untrue. The flesh of the deceased shrinks around the hair and nails, making them look longer. Humans perceive this change as growth.

are absorbed back into the body when they are no longer functional, making your complexion smooth and powdery. In addition, your skin no longer produces vitamin D when exposed to sunlight. Instead, the ultraviolet radiation in sunlight prevents the release of hemo-photon particles the epidermis emits as a by-product of processing vital energies from the blood; this can cause grave injury.

IMMUNE SYSTEM

You no longer need an immune system. Viruses and bacteria that find purchase in living hosts do not meet a friendly environment inside a vampire's body. The one notable exception is that the feet, moistened from the constant excretion of waste, are susceptible to the fungal infection tinea pedis, known colloquially as **night foot**, or to the warm as athlete's foot.

ENDOCRINE SYSTEM

Your endocrine system was formerly responsible for regulating the release of hormones in your body. Most of the glands (such as the pituitary) that made up this system all but burned themselves out in your rapid human-to-vampire transformation. Some, such as the adrenal gland, enlarged and are now constantly active, contributing to your enhanced reflexes and strength. The thyroid and parathyroid glands also enlarged, which gives you increased energy and aids in your rapid healing response.

MUSCULAR AND NERVOUS SYSTEMS

While a vampire's strength and reflexes have increased dramatically, their functionality has not changed at all.

REPRODUCTIVE SYSTEM

The reproductive system as you knew it is no longer functional. Your genitals are no longer necessary for you to procreate and can only perform sexually. Reproducing is now carried out by allowing a victim to feed on you. A vampire is technically of **three parents**: a human mother, a human father, and the vampire who turned him. All those responsible passed on the genetic materials that make up you as an individual. The vampire's genetic material—its particular strengths and weaknesses—have been passed on to you via the blood consumed to initiate the turning.

Where Did You Come From?

In all the confusion and excitement that has occurred since your body improved, you may be a little hazy about how you actually became a vampire. Here is what happened.

Your would-be mentor began by draining you of most of your blood. When you were weakened and on the verge of death, the vampire opened a vein of his own and allowed you to feed on him. The vampire's blood, which now also included a good deal of your blood, entered your system and began to work on your human body. Within four hours, a new vampire was born.

SKELETAL SYSTEM

Your bone marrow has disappeared, meaning that you no longer produce your own blood. This makes you lighter and able to jump higher.

RESPIRATORY SYSTEM

Your body no longer needs oxygen in order to function, and you no longer need to breathe. Your lungs operate on a purely voluntary basis, and are used primarily to allow you to mimic humans, to speak, or perhaps to smoke, for dramatic effect.

2

YOUR NEW POWERS

IN ORDER TO SLAKE your newfound thirst, your body has undergone a series of changes that radically elevate your predatory capabilities. As you settle into your superior form, you will marvel that you were ever able to get along as a human.

A word of caution: the dawning awareness of your enhanced abilities can be initially disorienting, then ultimately intoxicating. Many vampires go through a delusional period early on. They confuse superior with invulnerable and behave recklessly until they either realize their limitations or perish following an act of supreme foolishness.

STRENGTH

Your feeble human form may have been hard-pressed to lift a case of beer without wheezing, but a vampire can lift a car over his head with ease. Increased strength also endows you with the ability to

HUMAN   VAMPIRE

jump great distances and climb vertical surfaces utilizing minimal hand- and footholds.

SPEED AND HEIGHTENED REFLEXES

On average, vampires can move twice as fast as humans, enabling them to chase down any prey with ease. When necessary, **microbursts** of incredible speed are also possible, though they require a great deal more energy. Your reaction times are also decreased, making it much easier to dodge a clumsily wielded stake aimed for the heart.

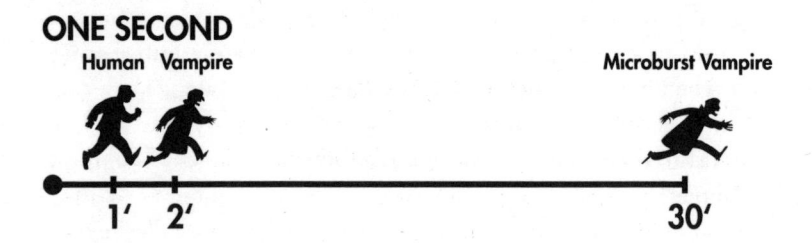

ONE SECOND

Human Vampire   Microburst Vampire

1'   2'   30'

HEIGHTENED SENSES

Increased speed and strength alone will not help you find your way around in pitch-blackness. Fortunately, with your new body, the night comes alive. You now possess superior night vision on the level of the cat, which allows you to penetrate the darkness with

> **MILES SAYS:**
> In my first year as a vampire, I was vain and foolhardy. So overjoyed was I to be a vampire that I acted without regard for my own safety. After feeding on a delicious morsel in the woods one night, I decided to stay up and watch the sunrise. After all, I felt the unfamiliar rush of power that a feeding brings to new vampires, and I thought that it couldn't be as bad as Zlatan had warned me. Fortunately, he found me just in the nick of time and dragged me into a hollow tree large enough to protect both of us from the rising sun. The first rays of the sun scorched my hand as he pulled me inside the tree, teaching me a valuable lesson I remember every time I look at the scar that never healed quite right.

ease. With your owl-like hearing, you can hear a jugular vein pulsing from yards away. Like the wolf, you can smell the delicious fear coming in waves off a victim. When you taste your victim's blood, you will be able to identify his blood type, what he had for his last meal, and what prescription and nonprescription medications he was taking. Only your sense of touch will be unchanged—which, admittedly, is a bit of a letdown after the dramatic increase in the other senses.

MIND CONTROL

The ability to hold sway over the warm is difficult to master because it is completely new and alien. You lifted objects as a human, so lifting heavier objects is not hard to understand; it is probable, however, that you never controlled another human's mind. When it happens to you, it will come as a surprise. One minute you'll be thinking of how distasteful it is that someone is a smoker, and the next minute you'll watch that person crumple up his pack of cigarettes, never to smoke again. After this happens for a fifth time, you'll start to understand and appreciate the causality, and you can work on honing your abilities for a greater purpose.

> ### Where Hypnosis Comes In Handy
>
> Once you get accustomed to the idea of controlling people and clouding their minds, the question becomes what to do with the ability. Here are some beginner applications.
> - Forcing someone to leave his house
> - Making victims forget they have been fed on
> - Causing a witness to believe he killed your victim
> - Convincing a cashier that your coupon has not expired
> - Getting a ride to the other side of town before sunrise

All **mind control** requires is that you fix your concentrated gaze on a human while thinking about what you want him to do. If he looks into your eyes, he will bend to your will.* At your command, he will follow your orders, remember what you tell him, or forget what he saw.

There are limitations. You cannot make people harm themselves. For example, you can command a victim to stay in position while you glide over to feed on him, but you cannot make him jump out a window or cut his wrists over a wine glass so that you can drink the blood in a sophisticated manner. The longer you control a human, the weaker his grasp of sanity becomes, so unless you want a gibbering fool on your hands, do not control one human mind for longer than is necessary.

CONTROL OVER ANIMALS

In addition to controlling humans, you will be able to communicate with and control certain types of animals. The type of creature varies from vampire to vampire. Most can control rats, while others

---

*Some humans are resistant to mind control. If you find one that is, it is best to seek a more compliant meal elsewhere.

> **MILES SAYS:**
> As I have gotten older, my ability to put humans into a deep trance state has improved dramatically. The number of people I can hold sway over and the distance at which I can do it has increased with every passing year. Now I can freeze a bustling sidewalk, disperse a small mob, or make an audience believe they have just heard the most inspiring speech of their lives. Nonetheless, I still use mind control primarily to feed on beautiful prey without getting caught. I plant a primary suggestion in the victim's mind that they drank too much and blacked out. As a precaution against discovery via regression therapy, I always plant a second, deeper hypnotic suggestion that the person had been abducted by aliens, and not fed on. It's an excellent red herring. If he uncovers that "memory," he usually doesn't seem very interested in delving any further.

have dominion over bats, wolves, or dogs. Older vampires can command multiple species.

> **MILES SAYS:**
> My command is over owls, which is a mixed bag. They are nocturnal, and able to send messages or fetch small items, but their temperament is quite disagreeable, and they disgorge some very unpleasant semidigested materials.

RAPID HEALING

Many humans labor under the false impression that the vampire cannot be harmed by anything but specialized weapons. This is untrue. Vampires can suffer a full spectrum of injuries, but heal incredibly quickly. While a vampire may be in a great deal of pain after getting hit by a car, he will be able to walk it off within minutes. There are exceptions to this rule (see chapter 3, "Weaknesses"), but

Dealing with a Severed Limb

If you lose a limb, it is very important to remain calm. Do not panic! Yes, it hurts, and yes, the prospect of going through eternity without a limb is terrifying, but nothing is worse than a one-armed vampire trying to exact revenge for the injury. The trick is to collect the severed limb before your wounded stump heals over. Retreat to safety and hold it in place. Within minutes, the limb should reattach itself enough so that you can let go of it. Full functionality will not return for twenty-four to forty-eight hours, depending on your access to fresh blood, but the limb should be useful enough to allow you to escape danger. It will be necessary to feed a great deal after this, so cancel your plans for a few nights.

Take care to align the limb correctly when you're reattaching it or it will heal improperly and will have to be cut off and reset.

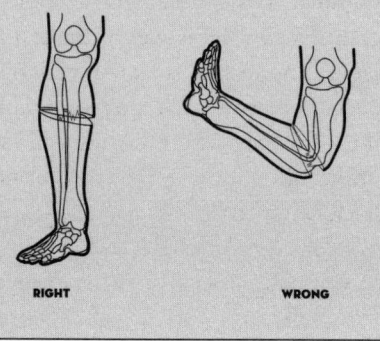

RIGHT **WRONG**

by and large, most cuts, punctures, and blunt-force traumas will not impede you for long.

LONGEVITY

As long as you stay out of sunlight and avoid having your heart impaled with a wooden stake, you will live forever.

A NOTE ON AGING

As you get older, some of your powers will increase. You will be able to control a wider variety of animals, lift heavier objects, and hypnotize larger groups of people.

You will also find that, around the one-hundred-year mark, new powers will begin to develop. The only reason they are being enumerated this early in your development is so that you know what to expect before you receive misinformation from another vampire. Don't be obsessed with these powers. They will develop in due course.

TRANSFORMATION

You will be able to alter the structure of your body so that you can assume two new physical forms, albeit for a brief period of time. The first is a bat, granting you the power of flight and the ability to crawl into small spaces. The second is a mist, which is useful for accessing secured spaces, but you can't carry anything. At first, the transformations take a few minutes, but they will eventually occur instantaneously. Clothes do not make the transformation with you, so when you turn back, you will be left naked and vulnerable. Make sure not to carry items of value or anything that may indicate the location of your lair if you plan on utilizing this power.

POWER X

At around the one-thousand-year mark, every vampire receives a power that is unique to him, called **power x**. It may be extremely advantageous or merely amusing. Some have reported the ability to move objects with their minds. Some can predict the future. Others can belch small flames on command. There is little advice to offer regarding this power, save that you must wait patiently for it.

WEAKNESSES

TO THE DISMAY of many vampires, your new strengths are accompanied by a whole new set of weaknesses. It is true that you will no longer find yourself laid up in bed with a stomach flu for days at a time, but after one inadvertent pass through a sunbeam, you'll wish for such pedestrian woes. These impediments are not insurmountable. Simple precautions can be taken to avoid them.

IRRITANTS

GARLIC

Garlic is very unpleasant to a vampire. The odor is noxious, often inducing gagging or retching. Like an allergy to MSG in humans, you will feel like you're breaking out in hives if someone cracks a clove of garlic in your vicinity.

THE SCIENCE: There are many theories as to why this simple foodstuff is repulsive to the vampire. The most common is that the pungent odor of the bulb is strongly associated with food and triggers latent human hunger urges. The vampire body, having evolved into its superior form, reacts strongly to squash those urges, often turning the body against itself. Unfortunately, this remains only a theory. No one wants to get close enough to garlic to conduct the experiments necessary for proof.

SLEEP

Like most creatures, vampires undergo regular periods of dormancy. Unlike other creatures, our loss of consciousness is nearly total. From sunrise to sunset, we slumber, and nothing is able to awaken us. There we lie, vulnerable to any predator that wishes to do us harm.

THE SCIENCE: In addition to the normal fatigue a body feels after a full night, ambient solar radiation interferes with the internal blood-

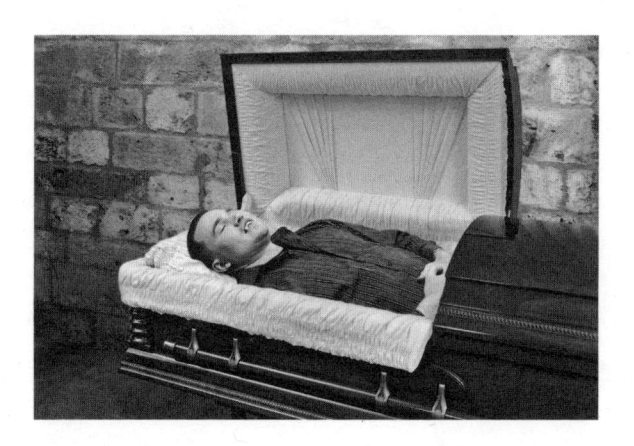

> ### 𝕎ill 𝔍 𝔇ream?
>
> Vampires do not dream because neural activity in the brain is greatly diminished during repose. This may seem sad at first, but you grow accustomed to it. There is no more replaying embarrassing moments from your adolescence or the kill that got away. Plus, instead of being confused and disoriented when you awaken, your awareness slowly grows with the break of dusk, until you are fully awake and ready to seize the night.

digestion process. As the sun rises, your body converts blood to energy more slowly, and it becomes more difficult to function. The body weakens and thoughts become cloudy. As soon as a state of repose is achieved, the mind closes to almost all external stimulus.

NO REFLECTION IN MIRRORS

No matter how hard you work to pass among the warm, one inadvertent stroll past a mirror will reveal your true nature. You may be able to brush aside inquiries by making up something about warped glass or plainly being able to see yourself, but the seed of doubt will be planted, and your nervous quarry will become more suspicious. Worse still is trying to seduce a human to feed on and being foiled

Light
Hemo-Photon Particles
SKIN
MIRROR

by messy hair or a smear of blood on your cheek. This is why it is ideal to have a grooming partner who can look you over and give you the all clear before you go out.

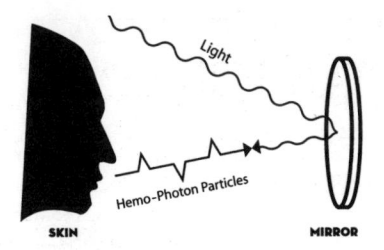

THE SCIENCE: An effect of the conversion of blood into energy is the release of the aforementioned hemo-photon particles from the skin. These particles nullify the light rays that would otherwise show up as your reflection.

INABILITY TO CROSS THRESHOLDS WITHOUT INVITATION

Try as you may, it is impossible to enter a house without first securing an invitation from a resident. Any attempt to do so will end disastrously.

THE SCIENCE: A human's dwelling is imbued with a familial aura that disrupts the vampire's stasis. The body is locked out by its inability to physically function within that space. (For information about overcoming this problem, see chapter 21, "Getting In: Invite-Only Buildings.")

COMPULSIVELY COUNTING SPILLED SEEDS OR GRAINS

This vulnerability has been all but forgotten in human lore, and there's a good reason for that. Vampires have worked hard for centuries to eradicate all knowledge of this obsessive behavior so that it cannot be used against them. There's nothing worse than chasing your prey and seeing him spill a bag of sunflower seeds he's been snacking on, because you are compelled to count each and every seed or grain before continuing. This is where autistic vampires have an advantage, as they can count the seeds at a glance without breaking stride. While this compulsion leaves you open to any of the attacks listed below, it's not fatal unto itself. It's simply very inconvenient and embarrassing.*

*This is why The Count from the children's program *Sesame Street* is such an affront to vampirekind.

THE SCIENCE: The prevailing wisdom on this subject is the Evolutionary Theory of Compulsive Counting.* In essence, it states that before books or other nocturnal diversions, vampires used to count small objects to keep their minds occupied. Often, they would count the smallest things of human value available to them, which were seeds, grains, and rice. These were all abundant, easily obtained, and useless to vampires as food. Over time, vampires who kept themselves from going mad with boredom and walking into the sun were the strongest counters. The counters thus had more offspring, who carried the trait, which eventually evolved into an outright compulsion.

PAIN INDUCERS

SILVER

Brushing up against silver stings, but the sensation fades. Firmly touching silver burns and leaves a faint red mark. Being cut with a silver knife hurts a great deal, and such a wound takes far longer to heal than one inflicted by a steel instrument. Fortunately, due to the proliferation of flatware alternatives—especially after silver prices

---

*As explained in the Vampire Graeme McGlynn's study *Biological and Psychological Rationales for Tallying Grains*.

skyrocketed—most people no longer keep real silverware on hand. People will always choose greed over safety.

THE SCIENCE: The cause of this weakness is twofold. First, silver conducts electricity better than any other metal, and ambient electrical energy is readily transferred through it, which temporarily interferes with our cellular regeneration. Compounding the damage, silver acts as a catalyst that oxidizes vampire flesh, which causes burns and diminishes the healing response.

FATALITIES

FIRE

Like most carbon-based things, you can be set ablaze. It's not as though your mortal life was spent in the midst of flames, so your vampire life should be no different in this regard. Trust your instincts and keep a safe distance from anything that is burning.

Sometimes, fire will be brandished against you as a weapon. This is where a cape comes in handy. It can keep flammable liquids from reaching your skin, and can be discarded quickly. Make sure it's wool, though, instead of the flashier silk or cheap polyester. Both are extremely flammable and will stick to the skin, igniting you like an undead candle for your last minutes on earth.

THE SCIENCE: Fire is a self-sustaining exothermic chemical reaction. It requires three things: oxygen, fuel, and heat. If all three of these elements are in place, a fire can result. This is known as the fire tetrahedron.

HEAT
CHEMICAL CHAIN REACTION
OXYGEN
O_2
FUEL

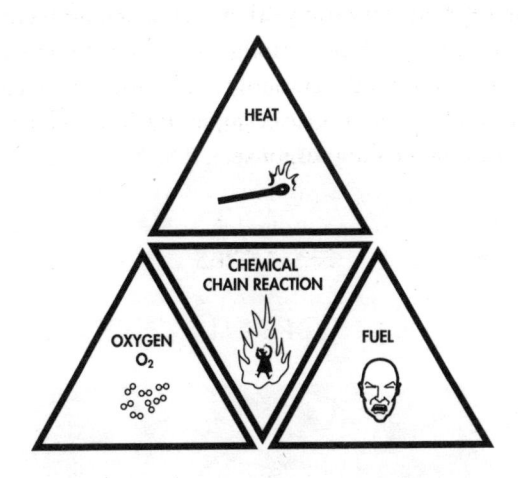

If any one component of the tetrahedron is removed, the fire will be extinguished. If you are on fire, you are the fuel, and you cannot remove that. The best bet for survival is to try to remove one of the other two components using a tried-and-true method: stop, drop, and roll.

A STAKE THROUGH THE HEART

A stake through the arm hurts, but heals quickly. Not so with a stake through the heart. Fortunately, the protective enclosure of the rib cage combined with a vampire's speed and agility makes a heart shot nearly impossible. Only when a vampire slumbers do people wielding stakes pose a real risk.

THE SCIENCE: Because of the heart's importance compared to other organs, a heart wound heals faster than a wound elsewhere on the body. When an object such as a bullet passes through the heart, the vampire lives because the trauma is minimized by this healing response. Ironically, this very healing response is what triggers fatality when the heart is struck with a stake. The healing process begins *around* the stake, sealing it in place. This causes a deformation in the heart's chambers, which ultimately leads to cardiac arrest and a painful death.

SUNLIGHT

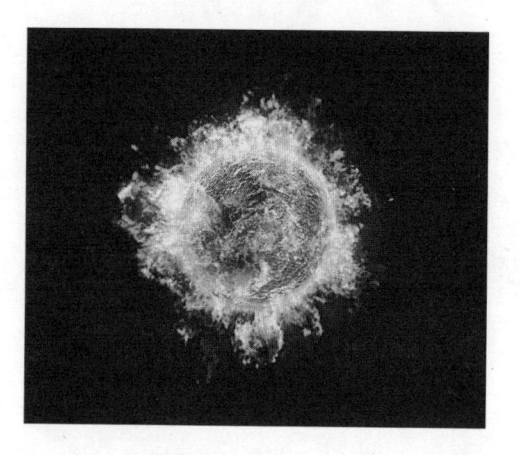

It is well known that vampires hunt at night because sunbeams will burn a vampire. This is why you must have returned to your lair well before the cock crows and the first rays of the sun pierce the horizon. There is little sympathy for the dawdling vampire who was so sure of himself that he wasn't safely ensconced in his resting place half an hour before sunrise.

THE SCIENCE: While ultraviolet radiation can cause burns or carcinomas on the skin of humans, it causes massive systemic disruption in

Myths

CRUCIFIXES
Holy relics, while perhaps distasteful to vampires, cannot be used to ward off a vampire. This misconception has been traced to a silver crucifix brandished by a German priest against the Vampire Friedrich Hoffsteder in the twelfth century. The crucifix made contact with the vampire, causing Hoffsteder to flee with a cross-shaped burn on his face. The priest incorrectly assumed that his faith and the significance of the symbol had driven the vampire away, and he lived long enough to give credence to that rumor among the villagers. The priest's faith didn't save him, however, when the two next crossed paths, ten years later. Hoffsteder ripped him limb from limb and drank from each of the stumps. By then, it was too late to quell the rumor, and the fallacy of the crucifix spread to holy water and other religious artifacts as well.

WOLFSBANE
Wolfsbane is excellent for keeping werewolves at bay, but, for some reason, humans misinterpret it to be an all-encompassing night-creature repellent. Good. The longer this misconception holds, the longer people will continue to hunt for it online, only to discover that it's useless to prevent us from savaging their wolfsbane-wreathed necks.

NEED TO SLEEP IN THE EARTH YOU WERE BURIED IN
For ages, the common notion was that a vampire had to sleep with dirt from the cemetery he was buried in. This was practiced for years, until the early first century, when a Roman guard was reborn as a vampire on the granite floor of a bathhouse. As he hadn't been buried, there was no dirt around him, so he just went on his way. Regardless, the myth persists in some quarters. Do not believe it. If you have to lie in a culvert until the sun goes down the next evening, do it. Don't try to beat the sunrise to get to your normal resting spot. It is an unnecessary and potentially dangerous risk.

CAN'T CROSS RUNNING WATER
One legend posits that the vampire cannot cross running water. Were this nonsense actually true, vampires would never have left the Continent, because what is the ocean but one massive body of water moved about by currents?

vampires. Brief exposure to UV rays results in the vampire's cellular fluids boiling, rupturing the cell walls and causing pain, discomfort, and ultimately death; all that's left behind is a smoldering pile of dust.

BEHEADING

No creature can survive without its head.

THE SCIENCE: No creature can survive without its head.

4

MORTAL ENEMIES

SHADOWS AND OBFUSCATION will protect the vampire only so much. Eventually someone will come forth to try to destroy you. The motives of these opponents vary. Some resent that you tower above them in the food chain. Some believe their lives will be better for having defeated a vampire. Whatever the reason, don't dismiss the danger these foes pose as weak or trivial. Study these enemies. Learn their ways. Your existence may depend on it.

VILLAGERS

Individually, the villager is not much of a threat. Chief among a villager's concerns is preparing his child for marriage, the weather, and how that weather will affect the turnip crop. He has neither the time nor the courage to hunt vampires on his own. The only real danger a villager poses is when his anger and helplessness reach a point where he bands together with others to form a torch-wielding mob for the express purpose of storming a vampire's lair to destroy him. To reduce potential conflict with local villagers, stay on good terms. Feed far from the nearest village and buy as many of their turnips as you can afford in order to win them over.

FIGHTING A MOB OF VILLAGERS

Appearing very frightening is an effective tactic to utilize against a village mob. Hiss loudly through bared fangs while throwing your arms high into the air.

MILES SAYS:

In my first hundred years as a vampire, I was quite taken with the villagers who lived closest to me. We had a very comfortable routine. Long periods of peaceful coexistence would be punctuated by a flurry of activity as soon as one of their kind disappeared at night. Anytime this happened, I would inevitably get the blame. The villagers would take up torches and approach my lair, whereupon I would do some simple thing that would scatter them into the night, screaming in horror. Usually, the missing villager would return unharmed in a few days' time, having gotten lost in the woods or realizing his mistake after running away to see the world without knowing the slightest thing about it. As for the villagers, I really couldn't begrudge them their pastime. They were confused and angry, and gathering into a torch-wielding mob was all the entertainment they had. It's just what they did to blow off steam.

Historically, this maneuver has been successful in creating panic. The lesser elements of the group scatter, leaving a more manageable number of opponents to deal with. In the carnage that follows, proceed from member to member and dispatch all with maximum speed.

Another strategy is to simply grab the nearest human and hurl him with all your might into the assembled throng. This serves the dual purpose of temporarily disabling a significant number of opponents and breaking up the crowd, which removes their tactical advantage.

REVENGE SEEKERS

It goes without saying that you will take several lives in the course of feeding. These incidents can usually be covered up so that the deaths appear to be from natural causes. On rare occasions, though, a family member will intuit the truth, and will take it upon himself to exact revenge. Clouded with grief, he will do a quick Internet search to learn about vampires, see what he has lying around the house that might work as a mallet, knock the legs off an old chair and sharpen them, and head out the door to hunt down the vampire who drained his loved one. It's easy to feel sorry for him, but don't. He will tell everyone that he is looking for vampires. Even if only one in one hundred believes him, it increases the anxiety felt by the general public. Simply put, a vocal revenge seeker is bad for business.

FIGHTING A REVENGE SEEKER

Should you get wind of a revenge seeker who has hunted for more than two days without getting bored, dispatch him quickly, but do not feed. Plant a grief-induced suicide note so that his next of kin will not go down a similar path.

Goodbye,
I leave tonight to
be with our beloved.
Life for me now is
empty, vapid, bare,
blank, vacant,
nInspired, weak, dull
and flat but I rejoice
that for you it continues
to be a fantastic blessing.
Rest assured, I was the one
responsible for my death so
don't go looking for any
one else to blam
Lov

SLAYERS

The popular perception is that slayers are superhuman beings graced with superior senses, speed, and strength, all of which are dedicated to vampire genocide. In reality, slayers are just normal humans, usually former revenge seekers who got lucky once and made it their life's mission to destroy vampires. Having encountered at least one vampire and lived, they now consider themselves experts. Don't let your guard down. Slayers definitely pose a threat. They are better armed, less terrified, and more intent on destroying you than an average human.

FIGHTING A SLAYER

While you outmatch slayers in strength and speed, their offensive and defensive arsenal is formidable. Their key weakness is cockiness, and after one or two kills, poise bloats into overconfidence. Catchphrases will fly alongside arrows initially, but when a slayer's supply of long-range weapons is depleted, that is the time to strike. Use your speed to overpower him as he reaches for a sidearm. Quickly and satisfyingly pull off the slayer's head mid-quip.

Do not simply plunge your fangs into a slayer's neck. Resist any temptation to feed, no matter how strong it may be. Many a vampire has been destroyed because he began a victorious feeding only to have a silver knife slid into his heart by a tenacious slayer.

Fake Slayers

No slayer survives long enough to become famous. You may hear names spoken in hushed tones—the Holy Wrath, the Sunbringer, and Loco are just a few—but don't be taken in. The best-known slayers are always actually vampires pretending to be mortals. On occasion, one of these frauds might cause several disappearances in a small but affluent community, leaving behind enough conspicuous evidence to indicate his presence. He will then approach an upstanding member of that community, posing as a mysterious human warrior with an impressive arsenal of weapons, and offer to rid the townspeople of their "vampire problem" for an exorbitant fee. Once the sum has been negotiated, he goes off on the "hunt," returning two nights later with a bloodied cape and burned skull fragments, claiming that this was all that remained of the vampire, and that their streets are now safe. He then takes the money and leaves town. This particular grift is called the Blake Switch.

WEREWOLVES

A werewolf is a human who, after surviving an attack from another werewolf, has been infected with lycanthropy. Werewolves assume many physical attributes of a wolf but are larger, stronger, and have greater animal cunning. Like vampires, they are dwellers of the night, but they are bound to the lunar cycle, transforming only under the full moon. During this time, it is best to be wary. Werewolves and vampires have always been mortal enemies because both compete for the same prey. Every encounter between the two will lead to violence and often the death of one or the other.

FIGHTING WEREWOLVES

Unfortunately, the vampire and the werewolf are physically equal. Werewolves feel pain, but then heal rapidly and are not quick to retreat. Hand-to-hand or close-quarters combat is not recommended. A silver bullet will kill a werewolf, but the consequences of an accidental discharge outweigh the benefit of carrying a firearm.

A werewolf's fur is highly combustible. If possible, set it on fire using a powerful accelerant. Something as simple as a well-thrown cup of gasoline and a match will often end a werewolf's night.

Also stay abreast of the specific times when lunar eclipses occur. A full eclipse briefly causes a werewolf to revert back to his human form, and a partial eclipse weakens him for its duration.

> **WORDS TO LIVE FOREVER BY:** When facing werewolves, the only real advantage a vampire has is intelligence. Don't fight stupid when you can win by fighting smart.

THE GRINNING MAN

Details about the Grinning Man's origins and powers are few, as no vampire has ever survived a direct encounter with him. Those who have seen him from a distance describe a male in a stylish white suit and report that to gaze upon his grin is like being caught in sunlight. He is universally feared by even the most powerful vampire. Your only response to seeing the Grinning Man should be to flee.

5

TIME

BOTH ON A NIGHTLY BASIS and across the expanse of eternity, time changes for a vampire.

TIME ON A NIGHTLY BASIS

The way humans and vampires perceive time is different. Humans abide by a timekeeping system based on the number 60. There are 60 seconds in a minute, 60 minutes in an hour. A vampire who continues to use the human system has substantially less waking time available, due to the fact that he must sleep during daylight hours. This disparity is dependent on geographic location and point in the calendar year, but generally most vampires switch to **vampire time** no matter where they reside.

Vampire time essentially doubles base 60 to a base 120. One human minute becomes two for a vampire and allows him to do

THE NEW VAMPIRE'S HANDBOOK

Nowhere is the time-perception differential more evident than when there is some distance between a vampire and his prey.

In this situation the human is always shocked and amazed at how quickly the vampire traversed the gap between them.

To the human, it was as if the vampire took only a moment to cross the room; she didn't even have time to react. To the vampire, however, it was several moments.

more with his waking time. Many vampires have their timepieces altered to help them make the change.*

The disparity between human and vampire time becomes especially apparent when a vampire employs his ability to move at fantastic speeds for short bursts. Such rapid movements are beyond what human senses can detect, so it appears that the vampire has simply jumped from one point to another. But the vampire is able to pack much more into the same interval.

Even though vampires are not subject to the same whims of mortality as humans, time is relevant. All vampires run the risk of changing to dust if they are not safely out of the sun by dawn. The relativity of time actually becomes heightened in this sense, and managing it is just as important for a vampire as a human.

One of the first steps in any attempt to effectively manage your time is to have a firm grasp of exactly when the next day's sunrise takes place. There are many different resources to turn to for predictions, but all vampires agree that there is no higher authority than the *Farmer's Almanac*.

TIME IN ETERNITY

For a vampire, time no longer passes differently depending on age. A human child perceives an hour as passing much more slowly than a fifty-year-old does. That convention disappears following the transformation. Not every vampire is chronologically the same age, but each stares at eternity with the same perspective no matter the physical appearance of his body.

Humans rarely consider eternity because it holds little significance; the finality of their lives keeps them primarily focused on the present. Thus comparatively little attention is paid to the life of the sun, or whether an asteroid can knock the earth off its axis. Most of

---

*Take your watch in and tell the watchmaker to double its pace. If he asks questions, just say it's because you're really, really late all the time.

humanity believes that the destruction of the earth is highly unlikely to happen during their short lifetimes; vampires understand the inevitability of such an event. For a thoughtful vampire, the end of life on earth hovers as a great storm cloud above a road with no end.

6

EXISTENTIAL CRISES

ONE MOMENT you're gleefully shredding the throat of an inattentive saleswoman. The next, you're lost in thought, with a mouthful of neck and a noseful of cheap perfume. Your feet are planted firmly on the floor, your fangs secure in the vein—but your mind is a million miles away.

It should be an enjoyable moment, but for some reason it isn't. The only thing you can focus on is the sound of your own voice, echoing inside your head as you wonder, *Who am I? What kind of wretch lives like this? Must I truly go on this way forever?* and, worst of all, *What sort of monster have I become?*

If this happens, you're experiencing an existential crisis, and you're not alone. Great vampires throughout the ages have experienced the same doubts, and grappled with the same questions.

Though you're no longer wrestling with the implications of your own mortality, there is a good chance you'll be wrestling with the lack of it. The prospect of an eternal existence naturally leads to even more questions about how to live it properly and, frankly, why to live it at all. The issue is one of purpose.

Did you know the purpose of human life before becoming a vampire? Chances are you did not. Then, one night, a bit like Gregor Samsa in Kafka's existential classic, "The Metamorphosis,"* you were turned into a vampire.

Now both existence and how you view it are entirely different. Unfortunately, while some of the issues that occupied you in your prior form have neatly resolved themselves, there are new, troubling matters you must come to grips with. The most relevant concern is that during the act of feeding, you will sometimes need to kill mortal innocents in order to live.

It is normal at first to question if your behavior makes you a murderer, if you are somehow evil. You may then wonder if there is even such a thing as good or evil, if there is a God, and, if so, if it is God's will that vampires exist. In order to grow more comfortable with your new and permanent state of being, you will find it helpful to choose a philosophical viewpoint through which to filter these misgivings.† Aim to do so quickly. The sooner you are able to accept what you have become, the sooner you will be able to enjoy feeding in a comfortable and guilt-free fashion. Modify the philosophy you

---

*"The Metamorphosis" is a story published by the Bohemian author Franz Kafka in 1915 that tells the tale of the traveling salesman Gregor Samsa, who awakes to find that he has inexplicably been turned into a large grotesque beetle overnight. Rather than shock or horror, Gregor's first thoughts concern how he will manage to get to work that morning. He is the sole breadwinner in his poor family, who, upon discovering him, make small attempts to aid him even though they are repulsed by him. Gradually their ambivalence is replaced with abject disgust, and Gregor ultimately dies from an infection that began when his father threw apples at him and one lodged in his exoskeleton. Upon Gregor's death, the family feels relieved of an enormous burden, and they begin to make plans for the future with a renewed sense of hope. "The Metamorphosis" has been adapted for the stage several times, and scored by such renowned artists as Nick Cave and Philip Glass.

Kafka spent much of his adult life depressed and ill, working in insurance. He also had a brief period of employment at an asbestos factory before he died, in 1924. Other notable works by him include *The Trial* and *The Castle*. If you would like to learn more about the fascinating life and compelling works of Franz Kafka, visit the Kafka Project, at http://www.kafka.org.

†Vampires who seek psychological help in dealing with these issues find it rather ineffective. It may take several sessions before you see improvement, and vampires are compelled to kill the therapist after revealing themselves in the first one.

> **MILES SAYS:**
> Years ago I attended a party hosted by the philosophy club at Northwestern University. I quickly zeroed in on an earnest, attractive young woman reading aloud to a small group of people in the corner. I thought she would make a good, easy feed, and turned my attentions to her as soon as she finished. In the course of our conversation, she told me about a book she'd been reading called **Atlas Shrugged**, written by Ayn Rand, and handed me her copy.
>
> In the book, Rand introduced a philosophy called Objectivism, which espoused a belief in self-actualization and a kind of moral absolutism that spoke to me. Objectivists hold rational thought and the pursuit of one's own good above all else, and have no regard for those trampled savagely underfoot in the process. This made solid sense to me as a vampire.
>
> Intrigued, I took a seat at the party and devoured the entire tome in one sitting. Rand was speaking my language. I felt I had discovered a worldview that resonated with me. I thanked the young woman who'd given me the book, and immediately put Rand's philosophies into practice by draining her that night. I haven't looked back since.

adhered to as a mortal to suit your new needs or abandon that belief system in favor of a new one more precisely tailored to the vampire's ways.

Fortunately, notable vampires throughout the ages have pondered these questions before you. While there is no one lens through which vampires must view the world or the unique vampiric condition, several conclusions by some of history's foremost immortal thinkers on the topic are represented in the following chart. However, the philosophy you ultimately choose to adhere to is entirely up to you.

NAME	PHILOSOPHY	NOTABLE QUOTE	UNUSUAL FACT
THE VAMPIRE DARIUS DUMONDE *Turned 1755*	**TOTALITY** One is not turned, but was always a vampire; the turning is merely the mechanism of the vampire soul's expression. Vampirism is predestined and is the highest aim and order of the human condition.	"A human is but a weak being, with flesh like clay; when it is sculpted by God, he becomes a vampire."	Believed that vampires were in fact favored messengers of the Judeo-Christian God and should kill sinners whenever possible. Dumonde is also considered to be a forefather of intelligent design.
THE VAMPIRE PIOTR ELASKYIEVICH *Turned 1861*	**CONTRITION** Be resigned to your fate as a vampire, but seek more human acceptance and understanding. Contritists believe that vampires will ultimately receive the same rights and privileges of humans but that patience, rather than bloody murder, is the key to achieving those goals.	"Through restraint, we assimilate. We cease to be monsters when we cease to define ourselves as such."	Elaskyievich's followers often utter one of two phrases to a victim before killing: "Mea culpa" or "Mea culpa, *Homo sapiens*."
THE VAMPIRE MERRILL T. COMFORT *Turned 1938*	**VOIDISM** The Vampire Comfort believed that a vampire should not only embrace his nature but exploit it to its fullest, even going so far as to kill at random to demonstrate his dominance over society.	"Immortality is a gift to those who own it, a burden to those who bestow it, and a curse to those who suffer its wrath."	Comfort was an out-of-work, alcoholic human drifter who enjoyed his vampirism immensely. He was murdered by other vampires when his outrageous egotism and cavalier killing became too much for them to bear.

7

VAMPIROSEXUALITY

ONE OF THE MORE jarring transitions newly turned vampires experience is the complete dissolution of their human sexual orientation. The questions that ensue shake one's sexual identity to its foundations. *Am I straight? Gay? Bi? Polyamorous? Is it just the hunger?* All seemingly valid questions. All truly irrelevant. The fact is, your new libidinous urges represent the end of sexuality as you know it. You are now **vampirosexual.**

To many new vampires, the urge to copulate is as unquenchable as it is nonsensical. After all, there is no impregnation during vampire-to-vampire sex. As with many quizzical aspects of our kind, there is evidence to suggest that sexual impulses are relics of our former breeding-prone selves. Of course, when it comes to sex, everything is more complicated.

The easiest way to understand vampirosexuality is to focus on what drove your carnal impulses as a human. Was it the desire to litter the world with a modified version of yourself? Maybe one to three times, but for the most part you probably tore off your clothes and got sweaty because it was a physical expression of how attractive, intelligent, funny, financially impressive, or well connected you found another person. The same is true for vampires, although in our case, alcohol is never involved.

Vampire coitus isn't simply about routinely reaching indescribable echelons of ecstasy; it's also about education. If a vampire enters his five hundredth year of existence, bleeds an entire NFL team, and controls the mind of the president all in the same night, his doorstep will be littered with suitors the following evening.* The reason for this comes down to basic survival. Vampires continue to thrive by studying the successful vampires of the present era. If you're close enough to have sex with a vampire, you're also close enough to learn from him. Vampirekind has simply applied the maxim of countless college sophomores and ambitious corporate underlings to our entire existence: Sleeping with your superiors gets you ahead.

> **WORDS TO LIVE FOREVER BY:** Vampirosexuality is not about the power of attraction. It is about the attraction of power.

THE SCIENCE OF VAMPIRE ATTRACTION

As with most species that engage in sexual relations, vampires are believed to be driven to seek out intercourse by chemical substances known as pheromones. The **hemo-libidinal exchange** is the process whereby **hemo-dense pheromones,** which are a by-product of only the highest-vitality blood, are received by a vampire and synthesized into arousing sensations.

---

*This trifecta of accomplishments nearly occurred in 1982, but unfortunately the Vampire Adam Truvell was unable to catch the Washington Redskins before their charter left for a game in Tampa Bay.

THE HEMO-LIBIDINAL EXCHANGE

1. The process begins when a vampire (noted here as Vampire Alpha) drinks high-vitality blood (see chapter 9, "Nourishment") from the throats of his many slain mortals.

2. The victims' blood is absorbed into Vampire Alpha's tissue. Parts of the high-vitality blood are converted into hemo-dense pheromones.

3. The hemo-dense pheromones are expressed through the mouth and shared with a nearby vampire (noted here as Vampire Beta).

4. Once airborne, the hemo-dense pheromones enter Vampire Beta through the nasal cavity and reach the part of the brain responsible for converting pheromones into neurological signals, which cause Vampire Beta to long for the wanton touch of the gifted Alpha.

5. Vampires Alpha and Beta exchange knowledge.

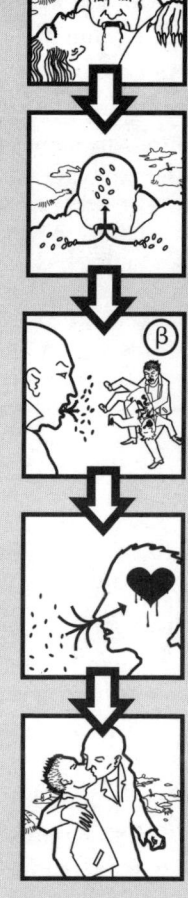

VAMPIROSEXUALITY AND GENDER IDENTITY

Sexual orientation, regardless of the corporeal status of the species, is difficult to definitively account for, given the many biological and

> **MILES SAYS:**
> My first vampirosexual experience was initially disconcerting because it was with another male vampire, which was not my preference as a mortal. The Vampire Didrik Mykland was a beautiful, hulking Norseman. I first laid eyes on him during a four-night feeding party in the Falklands—his flowing blond hair speckled with a smorgasbord of blood from Argentines, sheep, and British colonialists. I pined for him instantly and couldn't stop myself from fake-feeding on the jugular of an already drained sailor just to get closer to Didrik's piercing blue eyes. That night he took me into his arms and as soon as we touched my misgivings about what I thought was a homosexual experience were put to rest. There was no man-on-man sex. There was no man-on-woman sex. There was only Milos-on-Didrik sex, and it was good. He taught me a lot that night and was a forgiving lover. At one point I started to feed on him, having heard some vampires were into that kind of thing, but he quickly pushed me away, howling out, "Whoa there, freaky fangs. Not okay! Do I look Dutch to you?" The affair ended when the blood ran dry, but thanks to the Vampire Didrik, I left the islands having finally accepted and embraced my vampirosexuality. I still miss him.

social factors that drive an organism to prefer one gender over another. For vampires, reproduction has no relationship to gender or sexuality. The bulges, protrusions, and orifices that were once necessary for human procreation are now nothing more than cosmetic accessories. Both male and female vampires can turn—which is to say, give birth to—other vampires, and without this bold distinction between the genders, it would seem logical and natural that a pansexual outlook on life would develop. Vampires are but one gender. This is why vampires long ago did away with titles of Mr. and Mrs. and instead opted for the unisex title **the Vampire.**[*]

---

[*] The first use of "the Vampire" as an honorific dates back to A.D. 1054, when Corwin Lefebvre, of the Ruling Family Lefebvre, coined the term. Because of his long hair, smooth-cheeked face, waifish torso, and graceful legs, many victims spent their last breaths questioning his gender. Fed up with the perception of androgyny, Corwin demanded that victims address him simply as the Vampire Corwin, and in a show of support, the rest of the Lefebvre family adopted the title as well.

FANGS AND ORAL HYGIENE

YOU MAY HAVE cavalierly neglected your teeth as a mortal—going to bed without brushing, lying to the dentist about flossing, and jabbing at abscesses in your gums with peroxide-drenched toothpicks to avoid an insurance co-pay.

That is officially all over. Then you were in charge of your teeth. Now your teeth are in charge of you.

Unlike human teeth, which are made up of several layers of vulnerable tissue, vampire teeth are made of durable bone. There are no soft spots. You are no longer susceptible to tooth decay and will never need to suffer another root canal. However, your teeth are now your most important physical asset, and you will have to make an effort to keep them in top working order. To do so, you'll need to be aware of their basic structure and functionality.

> **MILES SAYS:**
> Since your first vampire fangs will pop the old human canines out of place, feel free to keep those as souvenirs of your turn date. I held on to mine, sealed them in resin, and eventually had them made into cuff links.

VAMPIRE "BABY FANGS"

By this time you will have experienced the growth of your preliminary vampire fangs, which generally arrive within an hour of turning. Much like your first human teeth, **vampire "baby fangs"** are temporary and serviceable—a new pair of razor-sharp upper cuspids that will allow you to take your first few meals and get a feel for feeding.

PERMANENT VAMPIRE TEETH

Within the next six months your full set of **permanent vampire teeth** will emerge, displacing the remaining human teeth as well as your baby fangs. It is an uncomfortable period, but unlike the drawn-out human baby-to-adult-teeth process, the vampire transition is concluded within a week. Even so, it's a good time to have around a companion willing to share his kills. For a few nights, you will be unable to break skin and feed yourself without the assistance of a pocketknife.

When your vampire teeth are finally complete, there will be some unexpected changes.

While chewing is no longer necessary, molars are still replicated so that face shape is retained. All of your nonfang front teeth will also be copied, even though they no longer serve their former functions. Now they exist for purely practical purposes, allowing you to

SOCIAL TEETH
RETRACTED FANGS
MOLARS
RETRACTED PIN TEETH
MOLARS
RETRACTED PIN TEETH
SOCIAL TEETH

FANGS
ELONGATED PIN TEETH

speak without a pronounced impediment and to laugh in public without causing revulsion or panic. These are known as your **social teeth.**

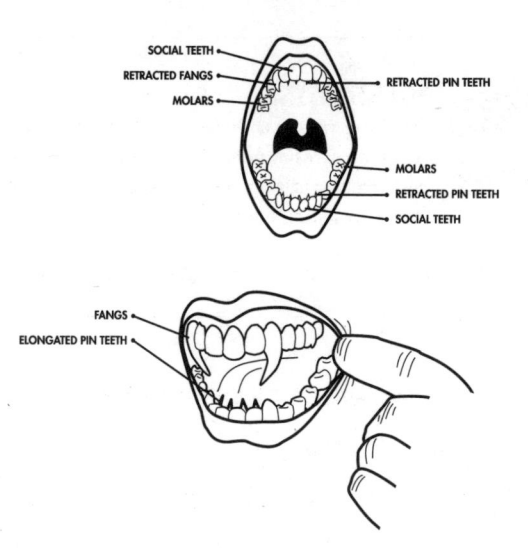

At first, the **permanent fangs** will not seem any more impressive than your starters, but they will when it comes time to feed. Moments before you plunge into a dockworker or night nurse, the fangs will elongate, going from a half inch in length to a throat-ripping one inch or more. Since baby fangs don't extend, some vampires panic the first time this transformation occurs, fearing they'll be stuck looking like a baboon for eternity. There's no need to worry; the fangs will retract to their dormant position within five minutes of a feeding's completion.

Another new development are two secondary rows of tiny spikes that take root behind the upper and lower front teeth. When you're killing, these **pin teeth** will also elongate, piercing two half-moons into the targeted area of flesh. The perforations created by the pin teeth make it easier to tear away the skin, giving you quicker and more efficient access to your food source. This is their only function. When not being utilized, the pin teeth remain retracted and concealed behind the social teeth.

MILES SAYS:
In 1936 I got hit square in the face with a steel beam and lost the bulk of my front teeth. I won't really get into the particulars, but it's one of the reasons I still hold a grudge against FDR and his New Deal. Until my new fangs appeared, I subsisted on the city's ample pigeon population, but had to climb over a lot of guano-coated gargoyles to get at their nests. It's not a memory I cherish, but I got by.

INJURY, REJUVENATION, AND MAINTENANCE

Just as your arms and legs can still be broken, your vampire teeth can be shattered during an altercation or an accident. Identical replacement teeth will sprout within a week,* but if one or both of your fangs are lost, you will not be able to feed in the conventional manner during that time.

It's important to gather a selection of tools to keep on hand for routine dental maintenance. Even though the instruments will be used to service all of your teeth, collectively they are commonly referred to as a **fang-care kit.** Fangs dull with use, so a good metal file is a must. You should also set up a regular filing regimen; once a month is usually sufficient.† The additional contents of your fang-care kit should be customized to your needs, depending on what sort of detritus you regularly find lodged between your teeth or clogging up your gums. Assemble a full kit for home, but also have a smaller essentials kit at the ready for when you need to travel.

---

*Since vampires have both two successive sets of teeth (making us diphyodont) as well as teeth that can regrow (making us polyphyodont), we are in a new dental category called **vampirodont.**
†Do not worry about shaving off too much of a fang while filing. Your body perceives filing as an injury, and it will regrow teeth as necessary to maintain a consistent length.

HEALTH AND WELFARE

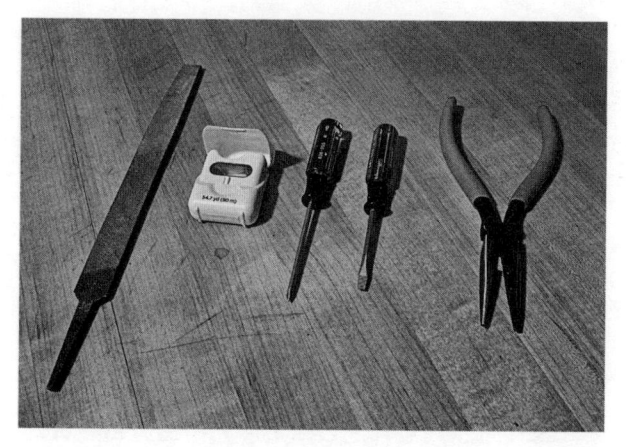

A typical fang-care kit for the home

WORDS TO LIVE FOREVER BY: Always file in one direction, never side to side. Your fangs will maintain perfection for tearing through a hide!

Vampires must also concern themselves with the issue of halitosis. Instead of tartar buildup, you are at risk of suffering from platelet buildup on your teeth and gums. As anyone who has ever worked at a slaughterhouse knows, blood can produce a powerful, repugnant stench once it's coagulated and sat around for a while. Unless you proactively fight against it, this stench will permeate your mouth and stand in your way when it comes to luring better-bred victims and seducing humans. Bleach is ultimately the best remedy for this problem. Swish a half cup around the mouth before retiring each dawn. While bleach is no longer toxic to your system like it used to be, take special care not to swallow. As with any non-blood substance, ingestion will result in immediate and sometimes violent regurgitation.

FEEDING

9

NOURISHMENT

NUTRITIONAL NEEDS VARY from vampire to vampire, but a general guideline is to feed until your hunger is satisfied. For most, this means consuming up to six pints of fresh blood a night.

Your hunger will tell you when to feed, but how much blood you require is another matter. Vampires have no army of nutritionists to stroke their chins and revise dietary recommendations every decade.

HOW MUCH DO I NEED TO FEED?

- The amount of blood vitality required by a fledgling vampire is much higher due to the numerous transformations your body is undergoing.
- Make sure the victims you feed from are relatively healthy. The healthier a victim, the more vital his blood. **High-vitality blood** is more sustaining, and a vampire can make due with less.
- Avoid feeding from drug addicts, alcoholics, and paint

General Nightly Blood Consumption, by Age

AGE IN YEARS	RECOMMENDED BLOOD CONSUMPTION
1 to 4	6 pints
5 to 20	5.5 pints
21 to 100	5.25 pints
101 to 200	5 pints
201 to 300	4.5 pints
301 to 400	3.75 pints
401 to 500	2.75 pints
501 and over	1 pint

huffers. The presence of contaminants diminishes their blood vitality.
- It's possible to work up a powerful hunger if you've been exerting yourself. Be ready to satiate it.
- The amount of blood required to facilitate regeneration depends on the severity of the injury. You may need more after a battle or minor exposure to the sun.
- One can manage with bagged or packaged blood, but it lacks the full vitality of fresh blood. For this reason, an additional pint is usually in order. (For subsistence on animal blood, see chapter 12, "Animaltarianism.")
- Try not to skip feedings. Without a nightly intake of blood, a vampire's body will start to wither. Your hunger can become so powerful that it overtakes you. It's better to maintain a regular schedule than try to play catch-up. That way you're not tempted to go into a grocery store and feed on everyone in sight.

Some Common Side Effects of Blood Starvation

In the event that you are unable to feed for a stretch of time, expect initial discomfort and then progressively more serious side effects.

TIME	SIDE EFFECT
1 night	Jaw ache, sensitivity to all light, irritability
3 nights	Sluggishness, difficulty arising, decreased mental performance
5 nights	Weakness, shaking, dwindling memory
7 nights	Distended fangs, paralysis, total loss of higher brain functions

OVERFEEDING

Just as all vampires do not need the same amount of blood to survive, not all can safely consume the same amount. Your hunger not only serves as an alert that your body needs nourishment but also functions as a shutoff mechanism. The absence of hunger means that your nutritive needs have been met. Going past that point is **overfeeding.** The best way to avoid it is to recognize the difference between bloodlust and a healthy lust for life.

Bloodlust is a preoccupation with the thrilling, titillating rush of feeding, such as experiencing feelings of power or, simply, a fascination with gore. Most vampires at one time or another experience bloodlust and feed past the point of satiety. To do so is not an egregious fault, but if left unchecked bloodlust can become a major problem for any vampire.

Prolonged bloodlust can cause overfeeding to the point of developing **blood sweats,** a condition that occurs when a vampire's body becomes so saturated with blood that it can no longer process another drop. Excess blood then weeps from the vampire's skin. Blood sweats, besides being uncomfortable, can bring unwanted attention.

In contrast, a healthy lust for life acknowledges that blood is necessary for survival, but views it as a means to an end, not the be-all and end-all. A vampire's life is never measured by how much blood he can consume. Pay close attention to your hunger and it will never steer you wrong. Ignore your hunger and it may drive you to your doom.

10

SELECTING AND LURING PREY

PREY IS ANY human on which a vampire can feed, but there are major differences between humans that vampires *can* feed on and humans that vampires *should* feed on. In a perfect world, the physical beauty of our prey would always match the savory succulence of their blood, but sadly, that is a rare occurrence. Instead, vampires must primarily suck on the veins of humans who are good for only their nutritional value, technically classified as **Prey Type A,** and commonly referred to as **kills.** Kills are your daily bread. They are abundant and can be left for dead with little to no impact on their community. They exist in virtual anonymity and are ideal for low-profile killing. In total there are four grades of prey, shown in the chart below, but as a newly turned vampire, you must first master hunting this most basic group.

While the prey pyramid is a good guideline, kills are not always identifiable by looks alone. Occasionally a human's significance is not consistent with his or her appearance.* Therefore, all prey must

---

*This prey is called **Type B.** Though not known by the vast majority of people, their im-

Prey Classification Guide

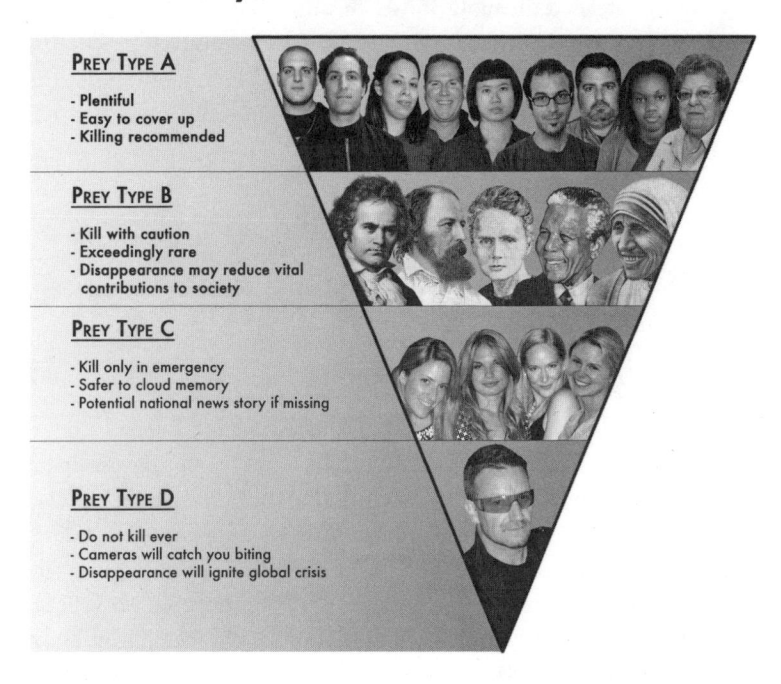

Prey Type A
- Plentiful
- Easy to cover up
- Killing recommended

Prey Type B
- Kill with caution
- Exceedingly rare
- Disappearance may reduce vital contributions to society

Prey Type C
- Kill only in emergency
- Safer to cloud memory
- Potential national news story if missing

Prey Type D
- Do not kill ever
- Cameras will catch you biting
- Disappearance will ignite global crisis

be screened through a regulatory process called **luring.** The paramount reason so much care should be exercised when killing a human for food is to prevent a dangerous condition known as **Hyperdracula Cognition,**[*] which is when the public becomes acutely aware of vampire activities. This state can be caused by several fac-

---

portant contributions to society in the fields of science, the arts, and politics may lead some to notice their disappearance.

[*]During the Hyperdracula Cognition Near Debacle of 1937, the Vampire Hubert Aggrid sneaked into the cargo hold of a plane departing Papua New Guinea with plans to feed on the pilot in midflight. Not realizing until after takeoff that the pilot was famed aviatrix Amelia Earhart, the Vampire Hubert had to pull off a veritable magic trick and make both her and the plane disappear to avoid having the icon tell the world about her vampire encounter.

tors, but as it pertains to luring, Hyperdracula Cognition results when vampires feed on high-profile or otherwise notable humans, categorized as **Prey Types B, C,** and **D,** whose mysterious deaths make for a compelling story of national import.

LURING PHASES

Luring is divided into three primary phases: *selection, seduction,* and *isolation.*

SELECTION PHASE

Acceptable kills belong, by and large, to a self-selecting group—buffoons who are blind to their own dullness and honestly believe they've found the one charming, interesting, and engaging being (i.e., you) who prefers to be with stale dolts (i.e., them). Even so, you've got to know where to find them. **Culling grounds** are where high concentrations of humans gather, and by observing how they interact with one another, a vampire can quickly determine who among the throng can go missing for months on end without anybody else noticing. These faceless souls are your kills—born to die so that you can live forever.

Visual indicators provide the first clue as to who is expendable. First, there is the **corner dweller,** often found at social gatherings because the host autofilled the wrong email address and inadvertently invited a distant acquaintance who shares the same first name as a close friend.

On urban sidewalk culling grounds, look for a clipboard wielder desperately asking passersby if they have a minute for an issue such as: Tibet, the environment, whales, gay rights, voter registration, or experimental theater funding.

Tourist attractions are superb culling grounds. At these places, look for abandoned children, fanny-packers, and anybody wearing a rucksack-and-winter-hat combination even though it's July.

FEEDING 63

Nobody will notice when he is gone. They don't even know he's there to begin with.

Even if people do notice his disappearance, they'll be so happy about it that they won't bother filing a missing persons report.

It will be at least a year and a half before anybody they know asks if they have been heard from lately.

SEDUCTION PHASE

During the seduction phase, a vampire mingles with meal candidates to assess whether the potential kill has any degree of noteworthiness. If none is detected, seduction takes place in order to set the stage for isolation.

If, during your conversation, any of the following quotes are heard, you should look for other dining options.

- "*People* magazine paid me three and a half million dollars for pictures of my baby."
- "My confirmation hearings for secretary of state are going very smoothly."
- "I am a blond female in college."
- "I am Bono."

Conversely, the quotes below often suggest a level of anonymity that allows you to safely begin seducing.

- "I guess I'd say my best friend is my pen pal in Lesotho."
- "Model trains are just a hobby right now, but I'm hoping to make it into a career."
- "I'm pretty busy this evening. It's my *Stargate* night."
- "I am a fan of Bono."

Suggested Regional Culling Grounds of the United States

REGION	CULLING GROUND	HELPFUL LURING TIP
Southwest	Frank Lloyd Wright's Taliesin West	Take the tour and listen up for anybody who starts bragging about how many FLW residences they're visiting this year.
Mid-Atlantic	The Jersey Shore	Avoid the men. They taste like cheap body spray.
Midwest	IKEA Schaumburg	Shoppers regularly go missing in the boxed-inventory section.
Rockies	Sundance Film Festival	Late-night screenings of arty Mongolian films are packed with lonely film geeks.
Southeast	Disney World	Any adult with no child by his or her side is safe to kill.
Pacific Northwest	Qwest Field	The noise of Seattle Seahawks fans safely drowns out the screams of your victims.
West Coast	Google headquarters	Hide at the bottom of the employees' ball pit.
Great Plains	Mount Rushmore	Anybody who asks which one Lincoln is is fair game.
South	Bourbon Street	Stick to the women who are booed when they lift up their tops.
New England	MIT	It is normal for students in labs to go unseen for days at a time. Use that to your advantage.
Appalachia	Anywhere	It's generally assumed and accepted that a missing person has been kidnapped by Hill People.

ISOLATION PHASE

After successfully seducing your kill, the task then becomes removing them from the culling ground and taking them to an area where you can safely bite them. To do this, a vampire must maintain the interest of the kill, often through physical interaction.

Gripping your prey's hand while enthusiastically endorsing the place where the two of you are going is a popular method for extracting more dim-witted mortals. With enough zealous encouragement, most kills will go into even the most hellacious of environments, since they rarely receive such attention.

If further enticement is needed, there is the **impressive-automobile extraction method** in which your kill is dazzled by the opportunity to catch a ride in your flashy sports car or on the back of your customized motorcycle. Once on board, let them comment ad nauseam about how cool your vehicle is. While deeply annoying, these activities distract meals from realizing that you're pulling into an abandoned slaughterhouse where they'll soon be drained of their miserable lives.

FIVE STEPS FOR A SUCCESSFUL FEEDING

STEP ONE: Once you have isolated a victim, you'll want to turn your focus to the attack itself. Be sure to attain a dominant position that offers a superior strike angle. Your strength is sufficient to overpower a victim, but the skilled vampire never uses force when persuasion will do the trick. Don't rush the encounter. The last thing you want is to find your fangs stuck up your prey's nasal cavity.

STEP TWO: Take a moment to find a reliable entry point on the body that will allow unrestricted access to the blood flow. Novices will want to limit themselves to puncturing the jugular vein or the carotid artery, which provides the easiest, fastest feedings. Both of these entry points are conveniently located on the neck.

With practice and experience, most vampires will uncover a host of new entry points and explore alternate positions they wouldn't have previously considered trying. Experimenting with style and technique will keep the act of feeding fresh and engaging.

INTERNAL JUGULAR
CAROTID ARTERY

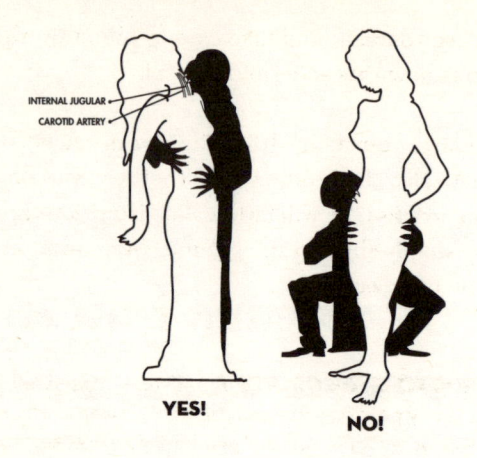

YES!   **NO!**

STEP THREE: Steadying the victim's neck or skull, use your fangs to pierce the skin and penetrate deep into the flesh. You should use a fluid but constant pressure until the desired puncture depth is achieved. The most common puncture technique, known as the **Kreislander method** (see following page), is to sink the teeth into the neck neatly and accurately. If this is a kill, you may also employ the pin teeth to shred a large swath of skin around the entry point, which will allow for unobstructed access to the vein.

STEP FOUR: Begin feeding. You will feel a short warming sensation as you drink, and a brief but intense energetic jolt. Some tingling may

Alternative Positions

also occur. Pace yourself, and take care to minimize the amount of blood that runs down the sides of the neck.

STEP FIVE: Remove your fangs from the victim's neck. They will retract automatically. Depending on whether you have killed or merely fed on a victim, he will either slide from your arms in a catatonic daze or simply thud to the ground. Step away from the body and vacate the premises.

> **WORDS TO LIVE FOREVER BY:** If you find yourself fumbling at any point in your approach, try making a little small talk with your victim. Ask about his favorite hobbies, television shows, or his tastes in popular music. Then, once you're both feeling a little more relaxed, savagely plunge your fangs into his neck.

Common Puncture Methods

KREISLANDER METHOD
The Bavarian Arnulf Kreislander developed his technique in the eleventh century through a long process of trial and error. Kreislander is credited first and foremost with shifting the preferred puncture point from the hard-to-reach heart to the more readily accessible neck. This was undertaken in large part because of his unfounded belief that tiny spirited *elbe* (elves) dwelled in the chest cavities of humans, and would attack any vampire who disturbed their slumber.

WERNER-KARTOFSKY APPLIED LACERATIVE TECHNIQUE
Hans Werner and Albert Kartofsky were two fourteenth-century Polish scholars bitten by the same vampire late one night while studying imbalances of the humors. They quickly deduced that the most effective way to bleed a victim was to utilize the pin teeth and fangs in tandem, inducing massive blood flow whether or not the puncture was a direct hit on an artery. They also erroneously believed that such a bloodletting would be advantageous to a living human medical patient.

GOUDET RUPTURE

The Goudet Rupture is named for the Vampire Pierre Goudet, who was active in the Ivory Coast during the nineteenth century. He was known for his stealth, quickness, and unparalleled intensity during an attack. The method essentially involves creating a large gaping throat wound and slurping out the contents of a victim's veins. Goudet was received poorly by his contemporaries, and his method was considered crude, inferior, and extremely messy. In time, however, Goudet's undeniable success as a vampire became his own best defense, and today his innovations are widely imitated.

KORINE'S SOCIAL STYLE

Anna Korine was a lovely young South Carolina socialite turned in 1840. Korine possessed an unusually prominent set of social teeth, which she incorporated with great relish in her feedings. By gnashing deeply into her victim's neck, Korine was able to effectively utilize her social teeth as a secondary set of fangs. Though it was predicated on her peculiar anatomy and could not be learned or adopted by others, Korine's stylish method was reportedly a joy to watch. Her feedings fascinated and delighted the vampires of her time, earning her a great deal of affection and ensuring her place in feeding history.

12

ANIMALTARIANISM

AT ONE TIME, the thought of a vampire actively choosing to drink the blood of animals over the blood of humans was abhorrent. It meant turning one's back on the very thing that defined being a vampire and was considered an affront to thousands of years of culture. Times have changed, and though still outnumbered by the mainstream, there is a growing population of vampires who eschew the consumption of human blood and instead practice **animaltarianism.**

At some point in their existence, all vampires must resort to feeding on animals. Usually it is during a time of great duress, such as after receiving a serious injury to the fangs or when trapped in the sewers, where only rats are available. However, there are those who choose to do so for purportedly ethical reasons.

Animaltarians maintain that since we came from humans, it is wrong to feed on them. Second, they believe that because the reproductive cycle of a human is much longer than that of most lower animals, they are not a good use of natural resources.

This practice ignores several biological and evolutionary realities. First of all, vampires are, by nature, drinkers of human blood. Our bodies are eminently suited to overcoming humans. On lower animals, your natural advantages are negated. Most beasts are often more work to feed on, as they match or exceed our speed and strength. And except for those you can control, you cannot make animals stand still so you can drink their blood. Try hypnotizing a raccoon when you're hungry if you want to test this out. You'll find that it's simply Vampire versus Nature, with all the accompanying claws, teeth, and hooves that such a struggle entails.

As for the second argument, one needn't kill humans in order to feed on them. With many animals, you have to drain them completely, so any resource-conservation gains that result from human abstention are nullified.

Finally, neither reason takes into consideration how good human blood tastes and how good it feels for a vampire to drink it.

Even in the face of these facts, there are those who choose to sustain themselves without drinking from a human. It is for these vampires that the following information is presented.

As a guideline, the smaller and more biologically removed from humanity the animal is, the more of them one needs. Consult the following chart to see how much of each species you will need to consume to survive.

> **MILES SAYS:**
> I was once forced to take refuge in the Brookfield Zoo's children's zoo, in suburban Chicago. I was able to avoid detection and rejuvenate by feeding off the dozens of goats kept in the structure without killing any of them. However, when a goat I had been feeding upon during my stay collapsed from blood loss atop a screaming three-year-old, officials shut down the petting zoo and began to investigate. Fearing discovery, I was forced to pack up that very night and seek shelter elsewhere.

FEEDING

ANIMAL	SERVING SIZE	TASTE	ADVANTAGES	DISADVANTAGES
Rat	15 medium-sized rats	Thin, rancid	Plentiful, no risk of extinction.	Disgusting; small brain belies uncrushable instinct to survive.
Cat	2 to 3	Loose, vinegary	Easily found in both urban and rural environments.	Crabby; uncooperative; will bite back.
Opossum	2	Clotted, spoiled	They usually play dead if approached.	They don't always play dead if approached.
Dog	1 large dog	Runny, meaty	Often tied up outside.	Humans react more strongly to the sight of a vampire feeding on a dog than one feeding on another human.
Horse	One-half to two-thirds	Heavy, grassy	Needn't be killed for sustenance.	Unless penned, can be difficult to catch; when penned, may deliver wicked kick to head.
Cow	One-half	Stiff, leathery	Easy to locate; too dumb to run; don't have to leave mangled corpse behind.	Disturbed herd might alert angry farmer; habitat is filled with effluvia associated with the cow.
Bear	One-fifth	Viscous, gamy	Imbues drinker with sufficient strength.	Hard to find, and when you do, it's still a bear.

13

DISASTER PREPAREDNESS

IN THE BLINK OF AN EYE, floods, fires, and hurricanes can wreak enormous havoc—and present the feeding opportunity of a lifetime. Imagine an unparalleled selection of vulnerable, disoriented prey, aimlessly roaming deserted, rubble-filled streets, or the melee of a frenzied, chaotic crowd of people running for their lives as a fiery city collapses like a house of cards behind them. Envision an environment where scores of mangled, blood-drained bodies are nothing out of the ordinary and don't even raise a modicum of suspicion. These situations offer a hungry vampire all the convenience and delight of an all-you-can-eat buffet.

> **WORDS TO LIVE FOREVER BY:** When disaster strikes, so do you. Act fast and take advantage of a cataclysm as soon as you can.

FEEDING

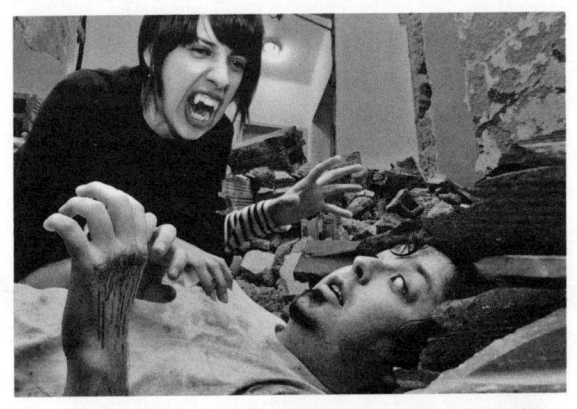

Of course, every disaster is unique, and the bounty will vary depending on the type and location of the diasaster. The important thing is to be prepared. If you're ready to act when chaos is headed your way, you'll be in an enviable position regardless.

> **MILES SAYS:**
>
> In 1883, Zlatan and I headed to the South Seas island of Krakatoa when the formidable eponymous volcano began to erupt. Zlatan wasted no time in taking advantage of the chaos left in the volcano's wake, but instead of hurrying off behind him, I hung back on the nearby Indonesian atoll we were using as a base to stalk a lovely nubile island native I had become infatuated with. "I'll go tomorrow," I said. The next night I said the same thing, and the night after that.
>
> But Krakatoa was no ordinary volcano. It erupted for several days and was among the loudest, most powerful, and most epic events ever recorded. In the end, more than 36,000 people died—and not one of them by my hands. Sure, I finally drained the girl I'd had my eye on, but frankly, it was kind of anticlimactic. By the time I finally got to Krakatoa, everything had been picked over, and the only humans left were already charred to a crisp. A well-fed Zlatan mocked me the whole way home, and I learned a valuable lesson: no one victim, no matter how enticing, is worth missing a once-in-a-lifetime feeding opportunity.

EVALUATE YOUR LOCATION

Long before disaster hits, evaluate the ability of your location to withstand catastrophe. Do you currently live in an area prone to blizzards, drought, or flooding? Are you residing in an earthquake zone or an active volcanic region? If the answer is no, consider moving to one. You'll also want to take into account whether your town has a chemical manufacturing plant, a low police-to-citizens ratio, a propensity for general lawlessness, or any poorly designed evacuation protocols. For these reasons, New Orleans, Oakland, and Newark* have long been favorite spots for many American vampires who enjoy disaster feeding.

CHASING DANGER

No matter where disaster strikes, you'll always want to stay one step ahead of it. Monitor global reports for news of rapidly dropping barometric pressures and crumbling dams or other public works projects dangerously in need of repair. Well-to-do vampires may consider investing in more complex predictive equipment, such as a seismometer, but basic equipment and the immense amount of information available from NOAA's National Weather Service can be enormously helpful to even the most modest vampire.

> **WORDS TO LIVE FOREVER BY:** Always ensure your safety and survival during a disaster before jeopardizing that of others. Assess the structural integrity of your lair as soon as possible, and be sure to stop by a hospital for extra blood bags to fill while the blood is still flowing.

---

*Though Newark is not prone to natural disasters, its general lawlessness combined with New Jersey's high per capita ratio of Superfund sites makes it one of the most statistically dangerous places in the nation.

CHECKLIST

In any chaotic situation, you'll want to have certain basic items on hand so that you can make the most of the opportunity.

EMERGENCY FOOD SOURCE: While most disasters provide a ready source of food, some are so devastating* that in the immediate aftermath, a vampire may have trouble finding living humans to feed on. Domestic pets, isolated families that refused to evacuate their homes, and the occasional emergency worker make excellent nutritious substitutes until better, more regular sources can be located.

BATTERY-POWERED OR HAND-CRANK RADIO: Instructions and directives broadcast over the radio will help you figure out where live, healthy humans have been ordered to congregate, as well as the locations of large populations that have been stranded without the aid of police or the protection of the National Guard.

FLASHLIGHT WITH EXTRA BATTERIES: Flashlights are very heavy and excellent for knocking out witnesses to your feeding activities.

BAIT: Cans of cling peach halves, ravioli, and chunky beef stew are all excellent tools for luring people to your lair in the aftermath of a disaster. The cans can even be empty, so long as they appear sealed.

DUCT TAPE: Duct tape has a million uses and can fix just about anything. It can also be placed over a victim's mouth to muffle his or her screams. Always keep a few rolls on hand.

---

*Up to two million people are thought to have perished in the 1887 flooding of China's Huang He River. Due to the high number of casualties and the percentage of survivors who quickly contracted diseases in the wake of the flood, vampires were unable to feed, and also had to flee the region for the sake of survival.

A LIST OF IMPORTANT CONTACTS: Calamitous times call for a heightened level of selflessness and generosity on all our parts. Should you come across more victims than you can feed on alone, alert your vampire friends to your location.

STOCKPILES OF ALCOHOL, FIREARMS, AND CIGARETTES: If the disaster occurs on a large enough scale, it can be followed by a total societal collapse that will affect both vampires and humans. The smart vampire is always prepared for a return to the barter system.

14

ALLUDING TO YOUR IDENTITY FOR AMUSEMENT AND FRIVOLITY

FEEDING SHOULD ALWAYS BE A JOY, but sometimes a vampire may wish to add excitement to the undertaking. One of the most popular ways to spice up your feeding routine is to get into a campy spirit and toy with humans by seeing how close you can get to revealing your identity before they realize they're about to become a meal. It is the art of **allusion**.

Alluding to your identity, however, is a dangerous endeavor. There is always the risk that you will inadvertently reveal your true self. While that riskiness is no doubt part of the thrill, alluding is not something that should be taken up by the newly turned.* It takes years of studying prey behavior, and experienced vampires know that carrying out a successful allusion is far more complicated and difficult than it seems on the surface. These are not phrases one should be improvising in the moment. The more study and preparation you put into crafting allusions now, the more fun it will be to deliver them later.

---

*There is no defined age for when a vampire is ready to make allusions, but if you're still under the eighty-year mark, it is probably too soon.

THREE KEY COMPONENTS
OF A SUCCESSFUL ALLUSION

THE NIGHT

It's only fair to start hinting at your identity by pointing to the number one thing most humans know about vampires—namely, that we are nocturnal creatures.

Sample Phrases:

"I guess you might say I'm more of a . . . night person."

"Look at how beautiful the night sky is. Don't you just wish you could live under the stars forever and ever?"

"I try to stay out of the sun. So harmful to the skin, yes?"

DOUBLE-MEANING COMPLIMENT

By design, these phrases are somewhat nonsensical. The pleasure here comes from the look on the face of the involuntary blood donor as she struggles to find the appropriate response to your bizarre flattery. The ultimate coup de grâce occurs when a victim is so stunned and confounded that she fails to realize you're gorging on her veins.

Sample Phrases:

"It is a pleasure to meet you. I have heard you are a person of great . . . taste."

"You must come from a good family to have such strong bloodlines."

"You possess the kinds of qualities I could really sink my teeth into."

BITE-POINT ANATOMY

Calling attention to the area that you'll be piercing sends the excitement soaring. For a human to say any of these phrases would be

> **MILES SAYS:**
>
> Don't get too clever! Excessive wordplay can ruin a great game of "Guess Who's About to Die." I was **this close** to sticking my fangs into John Coltrane in 1961, but I blew it on an overly complex allusion. For six months I worked as a barback at the Village Vanguard, roaming the Bowery and living off the blood of beatniks. I was restocking the bar for the night as Coltrane warmed up onstage. In the middle of his sound check, he paused, looked lovingly around the room, and proclaimed, "You know, Miles, playing at night like this—it's a beautiful thing, you see? Day jobs . . . day jobs are for suckers, you know?" Unable to resist an opportunity for a clever hint, I yelled from the back of the house, "I'd say day jobs are for the sucked!" Coltrane said, "Huh?" Rattled, I said, "Like, people with day jobs—they're good to suck on." "Man, what the hell are you talking about?" he rightfully shot back. Lost in a downward spiral, I began to spill the beans about my true identity and became so flustered that I dropped a case of Cutty Sark. Thankfully, Vanguard owner Max Gordon was so angry at me for breaking the bottles that he fired me before I gave myself away entirely.

really creepy and suspicious,* and watching your soon-to-be victims squirm as they try to figure out what is going on is one of the great delights of eternal life.

Sample Phrases:

"The perfume on your neck is . . . intoxicating. May I come closer to smell?"

"My goodness, I would not expect such a mighty pulse on a wrist as delicate as yours."

"I would caress your bosom but I was taught never to play with my food."

---

*If you do hear your potential victim say anything similar to allusions you might use, consider finding a new mark. There is obviously something wrong with the individual, and there is no sport in tricking somebody who already lacks common sense.

VAGUENESS AND THE HUMAN CONDITION

Beyond the recreational aspect of making allusions, there is also a beneficial purpose. Sometimes the new vampire tries a direct approach with a victim, thinking that frankness will somehow simplify the process. It never happens. In fact, saying, "Hey, look, I got to level with you. I'm a vampire and you're about to die" only makes the situation more complicated. In fact, human panic levels rise as frankness increases, and the correlation between these panic levels and **bite difficulty*** is strikingly direct. To that end, avoid making direct statements about your identity or intentions. They tend to drive humans out of the room, often screaming. When this situation occurs, the already challenging task of feeding becomes compounded by the necessity to stifle shrieks of terror.

Effects of Direct Statements Regarding Vampiric Identity During Interactions with Mortals

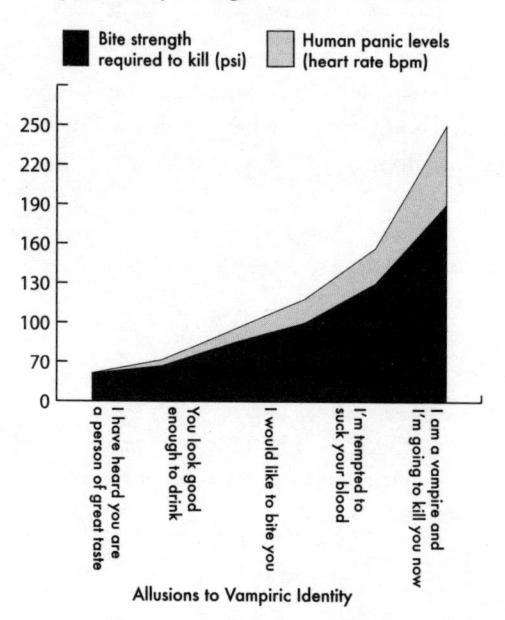

Bite strength required to kill (psi)
Human panic levels (heart rate bpm)
250
220
190
160
130
100
70
0
I have heard you are a person of great taste
You look good enough to drink
I would like to bite you
I'm tempted to suck your blood
I am a vampire and I'm going to kill you now
Allusions to Vampiric Identity

*Measured by the jaw strength required in pounds per square inch in order to hold down struggling prey.

VAMPIRE-HUMAN RELATIONS

15

A SPECIAL NOTE REGARDING HUMANS

WHAT ARE HUMANS to a vampire? To address this question, a vampire must look through a prism, for there is no single answer. The relationship is confusing, no matter how long you've walked the earth. They are food, they are family members, they are our inferiors, they are our former selves, they are hunters, they are the hunted, they are hated, and—sometimes—they are loved. You know from the previous chapter that revealing your vampiric identity is not without risk, yet you will learn that there are times when exposing your fangs to a human is a necessity.

Rather than viewing mortals as a monolith, consider each one individually. Walking down any sidewalk, country road, jungle trail, or sewage pipe, a vampire may encounter one human who has all the trappings of a fine slave strolling alongside another human who wobbles like a can of blood soup. Take each one as he comes.

16

VAMPIRE-HUMAN LOVE

SOMETIMES A HUMAN—a most uncommon human—will defy our expectations. Their smell begs us to kiss, not bite. The delicacy of their skin commands our reverence. The sweetness of their voice soars above the squawks and grumbles of the human rabble. You could, with a prick of your fangs, be with this singular creature for all time. Yet you restrain yourself. You fear that by turning your darling into a vampire, you will change the very thing about them you cannot resist: their humanity.

Against reason, against nature, against principle, you are in love with a human. To put it lightly, this is a complicated situation.

Vampire-human relationships are readily accepted in some circles and strongly forbidden in others. Removing issues of **vampiro-normative constructs** for a moment, there are several larger issues to consider before taking a mortal into your arms.

ON WOOING THE LIVING

For a vampire intoxicated by the touch of a human, the process of courting can be arduous. Our love is both instant and intense due to our animalistic pheromone-sensing abilities, which help us to know exactly what we're looking for in that special someone. We don't need to go through the complicated rituals of dating, flattering, and calling just to see how the day went. We simply want to run away with our dearest love to a place where no one can find us.

These peerless humans, though, are emotional, tempestuous, and flawed. They require a gentler, more traditional wooing. First, recognize what you cannot do for the sake of a relationship: namely, go to brunch. No matter how deep and abiding your love, it cannot place you in the sunshine of this popular late-morning/early-afternoon mimosa-soaked meal. In fact, even going to restaurants at night is a hellish prospect for vampires (see chapter 19, "Faking Your Way Through a Meal").

As for dating, try to think of activities that the object of your affection might enjoy that do not involve sharp objects. Should your beloved suffer an accident that causes an open wound, you'll be unable to control your bloodthirst. Stay away from ice-skating, group origami,* and couples' whittling.

Finally, regarding the more intimate facets of vampire-human relationships, it's important to exercise moderation. As a vampire, you have capabilities as a lover that no human sexual partner can match. A vampire's speed, agility, and eternal stamina endow him with certain talents in the bedroom. These talents should be put to good use, but not all the time. Treat them as gifts to be given on special occasions, such as anniversaries and birthdays. The reason for holding back is twofold. First, the energy expended during vigorous lovemaking can send your hunger into a frenzy, which in turn could put your human companion at grave risk. Second, on a romantic level, spacing out the supernatural sex sessions will help keep the spice in the relationship. These instructions are not meant to imply

---

*Even paper cuts can trigger your hunger.

Theories Behind Vampire-Human Love

No matter what species are involved in a relationship, science is always striving to understand love. Research on why some vampires choose the weak, warm-blooded embrace of a human over that of their own kind has yielded little results, but there are two predominant schools of thought on the subject.

THE THEORY OF PREVAMPIRIC VESTIGIAL EMOTIONS. Although turned vampires undergo a complete genetic transformation, the phenomenon of vampire-human love has led some to believe that **vestigial emotions** still exist in our genetic code. These trace elements of our former selves might enable us to feel the same about a human we once loved, even though post-turning they are only as useful as the blood they carry.

EROTIC AHEMOPHYXIATION FETISHISM. Hundreds of case studies have documented a peculiar sexual psychosis known as **erotic ahemophyxia**. For vampires who suffer from this condition, it is not the scent of blood that arouses them but, rather, resisting the scent of blood. As such, being intimate with a human while fighting the natural urge to drink of them is their ultimate fantasy. It goes without saying that this condition often leads to crippling and deadly hunger.

---

that you should be boring in bed, but sticking to a level of "skilled human lover" as opposed to "god-king of unyielding orgasmic pleasure" is advisable.

PRECAUTIONS

If, for whatever reason, you find yourself falling for a human, you must take certain precautions to ensure the safety of both yourself and your mortal partner.

Vampire-Human Marriage FAQs

As your relationship with a human progresses, it's likely that the subject of marriage will arise. Here is what you need to know.

CAN VAMPIRES AND HUMANS LEGALLY MARRY?
Our citizenship is only as good as the falsified identification documents that say we are human. In the eyes of the law, vampires do not exist. Therefore a vampire cannot legally marry unless he lives in the guise of a human. The question you must answer for yourself is whether being legally bound to your love is worth living your life as a lie.

CAN VAMPIRES AND HUMANS MARRY IN A RELIGIOUS SERVICE?
Some religions will permit matrimony between vampires and humans, but due to the peculiarities of those religions, it is unlikely that your mortal mate will be a parishioner. Also, if your beloved does happen to be a member of one of those churches and the marriage ceremony involves incantations to Pan, dancing to songs that consist only of screaming, or the use of raven heads, you should probably think long and hard about whether this is really the right person for you.

WHAT IF MY HUMAN SPOUSE WANTS CHILDREN?
Vampires cannot reproduce with humans. Couples who have tried are left with tattered wombs and broken hearts. Rumors of hybrids—so-called daywalkers—are simply that, rumors. Vampire-human couples do have plenty of options, though. If you prefer to raise a human child, you can always adopt; or if your spouse is comfortable with never getting to see their progeny grow up, you can turn a street urchin.

1. **TAKE IT SLOW.** It doesn't matter how passionate the love affair, never be in a rush to get serious until you've really gotten to know the human. You may be head over heels now, but what about in sixty years? Even if your shared love is able to overcome the increasingly creepy age difference, eventually your human mate will die and you could experience two hundred years of crippling grief.

2. **NO PDAS.** Public displays of affection can be annoying to vampires and humans alike. If a vampire who isn't as open to the idea of vampire-human love sees you kissing a neck he thinks you should be biting, you could be in for a prolonged conflict.

3. **ALWAYS WEAR A CONDOM.*** One would hope that in this epoch, wearing a condom would be a given but, sadly, many male vampires, being immune to STDs, fail to use protection. While you might not be able to catch whatever your human partner has, her body simply cannot handle what vampires discharge. Not only do you run the risk of ravaging your lover's innards, but the resulting trauma may cause her to think twice about the relationship.

---

*This applies to female vampires as well. While there is no denying the difficulty and discomfort of the female condom, it is a far better feeling than what you will experience if a nonblood foreign substance enters your body.

17

VAMPIRE FANATICS

EVER SINCE DEPICTIONS of fictionalized vampires began appearing across entertainment mediums, real vampires have discovered a simple truth: **vampire fanatics** are creepy. These Prey Type A humans are obsessed with vampirism as they have come to understand it through inaccurate pop culture portrayals. These bizarre people go around hoping and praying that anybody they spot with a wan complexion is a creature of the night. Unfortunately for actual vampires, occasionally they correctly identify our kind.* Upon first encountering a vampire fanatic, there is a temptation to exploit his or her particular brand of lunacy. It is understandable, given the unbridled adoration and extra rush of confidence a vampire feels upon realizing he is above reproach in the eyes of another. Inevitably, however, vampires come to their senses and see the relationship for what it truly is: a sick affiliation based on lies and psychoses.

*Often vampire fanatics think they've uncovered a vampire when in fact they have simply happened upon a **sanguinarian**, or a human who drinks blood. These mortal blood drinkers are truly loathsome individuals who not only disseminate misinformation about vampires but also waste our food supply.

> **WORD TO LIVE FOREVER BY:** These vampire fanatics don't love you. They love the idea of you.

Fanatics build up an idealized image in their minds of who you are. They see you not as an individual but, rather, as an epic symbol of infamy, sex appeal, and absolute power. Vampires should have a real, honest connection between themselves and the souls they slowly, methodically crush, but the second a vampire fanatic's unrealistic expectations of you are not met, he will bail on you in a huff and, worse yet, blog about it afterward.

While not physically irritating like garlic, vampire fanatics do have the ability to inflict a high degree of psychological discomfort. Their excessive unctuous flattery and constant morbid inquisitiveness can ruin any fantasy an attention-seeking vampire might have. Inappropriate assumptions fall into a few basic forms:

- Because you're a vampire, you must know every other vampire (e.g., "You think you can put me in touch with Dracula?"—overheard in Deva, Romania, 1921).
- You'll just feed on anybody, anytime (e.g., "Can I film you on my camera phone sucking my girlfriend's neck?"—overheard in Sisaket, Thailand, 2008).
- You are nothing more than a vampiric circus monkey who will perform on command (e.g., "Hey, turn into a bat! C'mon, turn into a bat!"—overheard in Los Angeles, California, 1987).
- You are some kind of sex addict who will fornicate with any willing participant (e.g., "Oh my God, you will not believe this, but my fiancé said if I ever met a vampire, I could have sex with him and it wouldn't count as cheating. Let's go up to my room!"—overheard in Cancún, Mexico, 1991).

The advisable course of action is to avoid these and other sycophants, but it is not always possible. They can be tenacious, badgering you with questions until their mouths go dry. Learn to recognize them before they spot you in order to avoid direct interaction. There are four common strains of the vampire fanatic.

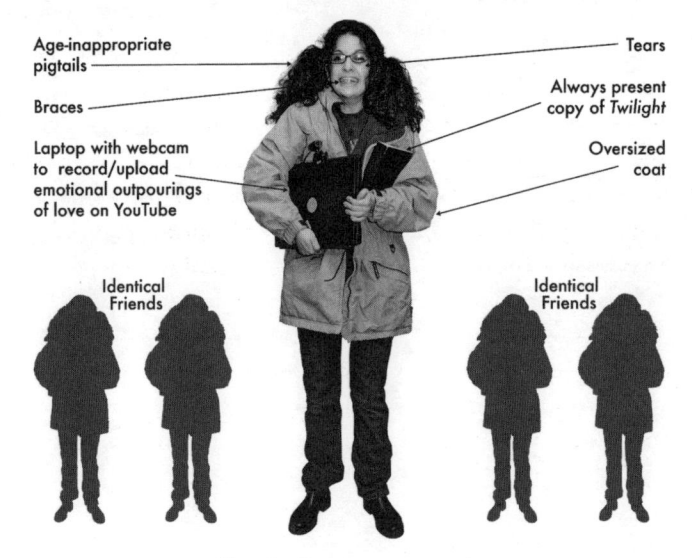

Vampire fanatic, tween strain

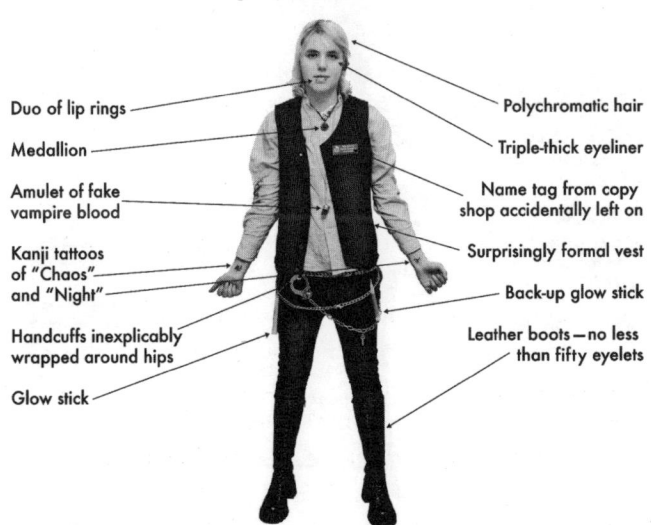

- Age-inappropriate pigtails
- Braces
- Laptop with webcam to record/upload emotional outpourings of love on YouTube
- Identical Friends
- Tears
- Always present copy of *Twilight*
- Oversized coat
- Identical Friends

Vampire fanatic, goth-punk strain

- Duo of lip rings
- Medallion
- Amulet of fake vampire blood
- Kanji tattoos of "Chaos" and "Night"
- Handcuffs inexplicably wrapped around hips
- Glow stick
- Polychromatic hair
- Triple-thick eyeliner
- Name tag from copy shop accidentally left on
- Surprisingly formal vest
- Back-up glow stick
- Leather boots—no less than fifty eyelets

THE NEW VAMPIRE'S HANDBOOK

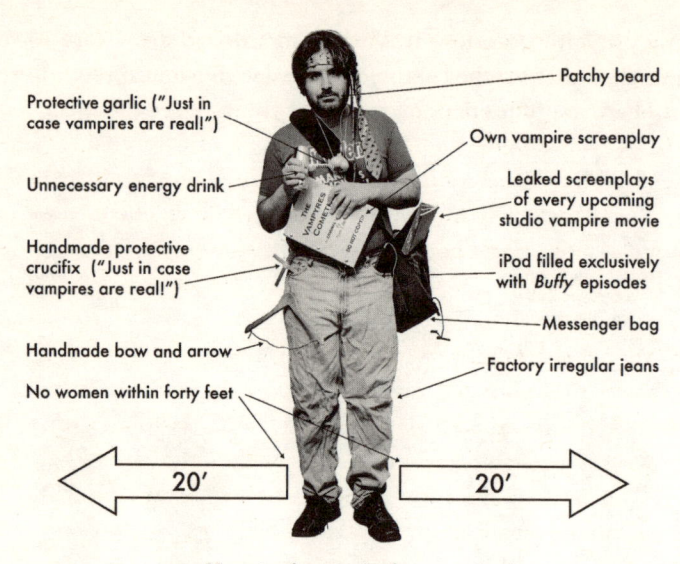

- Patchy beard
- Protective garlic ("Just in case vampires are real!")
- Own vampire screenplay
- Unnecessary energy drink
- Leaked screenplays of every upcoming studio vampire movie
- Handmade protective crucifix ("Just in case vampires are real!")
- iPod filled exclusively with *Buffy* episodes
- Messenger bag
- Handmade bow and arrow
- Factory irregular jeans
- No women within forty feet
- 20'
- 20'

Vampire fanatic, fanboy strain

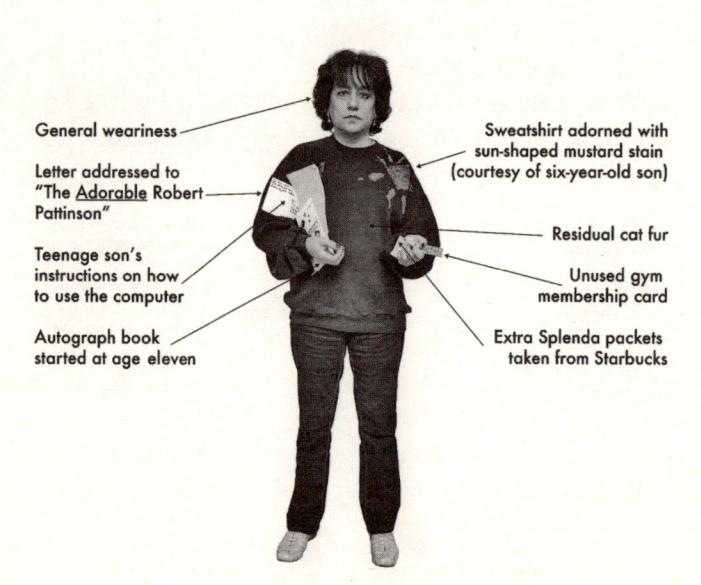

- General weariness
- Sweatshirt adorned with sun-shaped mustard stain (courtesy of six-year-old son)
- Letter addressed to "The <u>Adorable</u> Robert Pattinson"
- Residual cat fur
- Teenage son's instructions on how to use the computer
- Unused gym membership card
- Autograph book started at age eleven
- Extra Splenda packets taken from Starbucks

Vampire fanatic, mom-of-tween strain

The inevitable question is, What happens if you accidentally reveal yourself as a vampire to one of these sociopaths? It sounds implausible, but it does occur regularly. Perhaps a fanatic is spewing patently false vampire lore and the impulse to correct them overcomes you. Regardless of the circumstance, if you reveal yourself at a party or in a place of business or anywhere in which an expedient draining is not an option, there are still some ways you can deal with the situation.

- Shame the fanatic by proclaiming to everybody in the room that you told him you were a vampire and the gullible individual actually believed you. Assuming you are not at a vampire fanatic convention,* the assembled group will laugh at the fanatic and your admission will be viewed as nothing more than a joke.
- Act like you never said it. Then say something else unrelated. Then act like you didn't say that, either. Keep doing that until the fanatic thinks that either you're insane or they're insane.
- Quickly invent a fake trait about vampires that will turn the fanatic off. Say that we habitually quote lines from movies while still sitting in the audience, that we go bow-hunting for baby otters every spring, or that we love to sign up our significant others for hate-group mailing lists.

If you do accidentally reveal yourself to a fanatic, take comfort in the fact that there is a strong possibility that the human won't even believe you in the first place. Vampire fanatics think they know everything about us. If you explain how werewolves are our enemy, they'll give you an oral dissertation on why that is not true and how if you look at the vampire literary canon you'll see that the vampire-werewolf relationship, if it exists at all, has for the most part been

---

*For your own safety, stay away from Heidelberg in February, Houston in May, Glasgow in October, and Los Angeles in August.

cordial. If you tell them you don't have to sleep in the earth in which you were buried, they'll slap you for refuting their beloved tale *Nosferatu*. If you even dare to suggest that what they've heard about vampire weaknesses is balderdash, they will actually look at you with a straight face and say you haven't "done enough research on the subject." Though it may pain you to let their ignorance stand, it is nothing compared to the pain of being asked a barrage of insipid questions about what it's like to be a real vampire.

18

WHAT TO DO IF YOU SEE A HUMAN YOU KNEW DECADES AGO

WHILE IT MAY NOT OCCUR in the immediate future, you are bound to run into a human from your distant past sometime down the road. You'll be going about your business, and someone will suddenly call out your name. You won't immediately place the voice, but you'll notice someone frantically waving in your direction.

Your mind immediately smoothes wrinkles, lifts droops, and removes the gray from the hair, and the realization dawns on you that the caller was a friend from decades ago. Unlike you, he'll wear the ravages of age. How he knew it was you despite the fact that you hadn't aged at all is not important. What matters is how you explain the biological impossibility of your youth to him before he makes a scene.

There are several strategies you can employ in order to contain the situation.

1. Pretend you didn't hear the greeter. If you have already turned your head, act like you're working out a crick in your neck and not reacting to an external stimulus. Yes, this is an obvious, even trite maneuver, but on someone

that old, it might work. If eye contact was made, move on to method number two.
2. If he catches your eye and you feel some fondness toward the person, say you are your own daughter or son. Tell the person that you can understand the confusion, that many people say you look just like your parent all the time. Point to an invented difference, such as a slightly different hair color, a nonexistent scar, or a few inches in height. Make up a story about how the person he thought you were retired to Nevada a couple of years back. If the person you are talking to says he now lives in Nevada as well, tell him you meant New Mexico. Listen patiently about how great Nevada is, and promise to pass along any regards he wants to send. If this doesn't work, try the next method.
3. Sheepishly confirm that he's right, it is indeed you, but you just had plastic surgery. It's embarrassing; otherwise you would have mentioned it before. Add that no matter how great you look, you aren't the same person you were forty years ago. Your back aches something awful, and you have to get up to urinate at least twice a night. If this ruse meets with skepticism, move on to method four.
4. Use your powers of hypnosis to make him forget that he saw you. Explain that he is mistaken, and that you have never met before. Further, implant a warning that he will appear deluded and senile if he tells people that he saw someone from his distant past who hasn't aged a bit. If he appears destitute, the classy thing to do is to slip a fifty into his pocket before releasing him. If your powers of suggestion are somehow ineffective, move on to the final strategy.
5. Lure your former acquaintance away from all other people, promising to explain everything because, as an old friend, he deserves a good explanation. Once you're alone, tell him you're a vampire, kill him swiftly, and depart the scene immediately.

FAKING YOUR WAY THROUGH A MEAL

WHETHER YOU'RE PURSUING a warm-blooded amorous conquest, pitching a new business venture, or trying to convince a notary public to be on call from 9:00 P.M. to 3:00 A.M., a sit-down dinner may be required to seal the deal.

While the formal rules of dining etiquette still apply, as a vampire you face greater challenges than identifying the salad fork or remembering whether it's appropriate to eat asparagus with your fingers. As you now know, you can no longer consume the salad, the asparagus, or any food or beverage other than fresh blood.* Don't attempt to just force it down to save face, telling yourself you'll deal with the consequences later; your body will involuntarily force it right back onto the plate.

Complaining of a queasy stomach is an easy out, but it interferes with a dinner's social dynamic. Therefore, you need to stockpile an

---

*A few cultures feature dishes that are consumed while an animal is still alive, such as the ikizukuri-prepared sashimi in Japan. If you find yourself in one of those rare gastronomic situations, relax and drink freely from the beating hearts of the beasts in public.

A modern bit bag

arsenal of tricks, excuses, and dodges to avoid actually ingesting any of the food put in front of you.

Thanks to modern culinary diversity, pulling off a dining ruse is much easier than it was in the past.* While you can never anticipate every possible situation, this should serve as a foundation for safely and convincingly making it through a mealless meal.

FOOD DISPOSAL

The most common tactic is to simply push food around on your plate, every so often discreetly disposing of a serving. For this purpose, it's recommended that you always arrive wearing a proper jacket in which you've secured a **bit bag**. This food-disposal device allows you to tuck away small portions with very little chance of detection. Traditionally, bit bags were fashioned from calves' bladders, but today most vampires opt for stapling or sewing the more convenient resealable plastic baggie into the lining of a suit coat.

---

*A tragic historical case involved the Vampire Hirst, who in 1370 visited the Earl of Hereford to secure a land deal. When the host noticed Hirst merely pretending to nibble the coveted wild boar haunch he'd been served, the offended earl had him burned alive in the castle hearth.

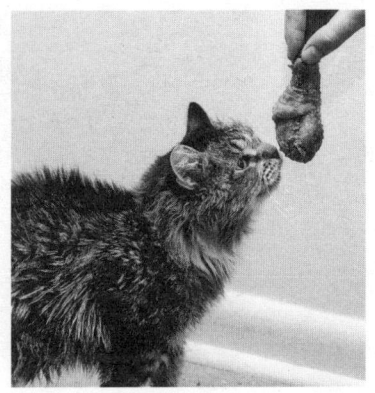

To ensure that your bit bag isn't bulging or overflowing by the time the entrée is served, keep an eye out for other opportunities to ditch inedibles. Arrange to be seated near something that can serve as a makeshift trash bin, such as a decorative vase, plant, or umbrella stand. This is best employed at a restaurant and not at a private residence. A host who discovers a cache of rotting shrimp in her home several days after your visit will not be forgiving. A pet in a private home can also be put to use. Even if you don't have control over the animal, once some meat is in play, the creature will become an eager accomplice.

Dinner Parties

Never accept an invitation to a dinner party. These meals involve too many people, and someone's judgmental eyes will always be on you, making it extremely difficult for you to control the situation. The only option in such a setting—frequently excusing yourself from the table to flush your meal serving by serving—can still lead to postdinner gossip. Even if the others in attendance merely speculate that you have a drug or gastrointestinal problem, it will invite further, unwanted scrutiny. Rather than deal with this tenuous situation, always RSVP in the negative and arrange to be out of town.

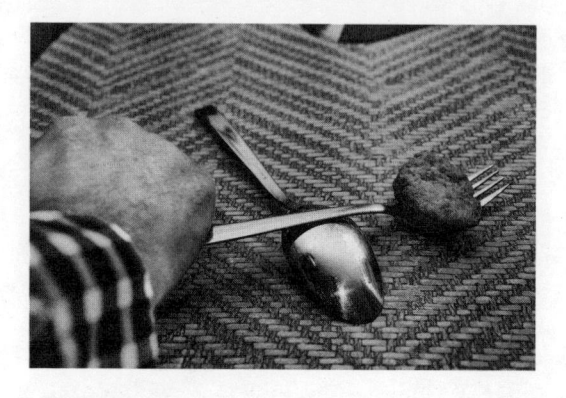

Your avoidance strategy can also be tailored to complement the purpose of the meal.

HUMAN DATES

Smitten, longing glances and rapt attention to your date's childhood stories can be used to distract him or her from the fact that you're not eating for only so long. If questioned, you can play the sympathy card and maintain that you have numerous food allergies, allowing you to eat only meals carefully prepared in your sterile kitchen. Just ensure that you arrive armed with an antihistamine injector for authenticity. When wooing someone with a mischievous streak, you might try spending the meal whimsically trying to feed yourself bites of your dinner via a spoon or fork catapult. It's nearly impossible to score a chunk in your mouth, even if you're actually trying. You'll avoid the food, but the reaction is a gamble. Your date will either find you spontaneous and adorable, or immature and disgusting.

BUSINESS DINNER

When a man sends his dish back to the kitchen, it demonstrates that he knows exactly what he wants and that he won't settle for less. Sending it back five or more times during the course of a two-hour dinner is the mark of a titan. If your companions are true businessmen, they will applaud your tenacity and immediately get behind whatever you are proposing, no matter how shady or sketchy the details. If at any time you start to feel bad for the affected waitstaff, it's also perfectly acceptable to change strategies and just ignore your meal while fiddling with a mobile communication device at the table.

CASUAL DINING

For "getting to know you" meals with a potential slave or other service employee, there are many religions with various dietary restrictions that you can claim to be a part of. With today's wide field of splinter faiths, it's simple to make up any reason at all why a meal can't be eaten. If it comes arranged in an elaborate vertical display, lament, "A broken tower, for the people of my faith, portends a month of sacrifice and hardship. So I must not eat for the preservation of their well-being." If your meal arrives regularly distributed on the plate, just say the same thing about its lack of height. Keep your stories marginally plausible, slightly profound, but nonconfirmable. This allows you to refuse food with limitless excuses while gauging your guest's tolerance of unconventional lifestyles.

Whatever the situation, if at any time your companions catch you in the act or start asking too many uncomfortable questions, just overturn the table and exit the venue screaming. They are far more apt to remember that than the fact that you were stuffing a salmon steak into your jacket.

20

AVOIDING THE MEDIA

DESPITE CENTURIES of careful construction and maintenance, the vampire veil of secrecy could be swept aside with frightening ease. If one piece of credible evidence was reported by the media, vampires would be exposed to an unending glare of scrutiny instead of continuing to reside in the dark corner of legend. The twenty-four-hour news cycle of the information age has increased the danger of exposure.

The citizen journalist phenomenon has further lowered the margin for error. Members of the media no longer bear such identifying characteristics as a camera around the neck or a press badge; they can be as anonymous as you are. Any careless revelation on your part could be seized upon by just one of them and disseminated in a matter of minutes to a potential worldwide audience from a never-ending pile of digital devices. Add the threat of increasingly omnipresent security cameras and the shadows shrink even further.

These new challenges are formidable but not insurmountable. Using commonsense precautions and keeping a calm, sensible head in a crisis will help prevent calamity.

The Báthory Story

The specter of discovery by the media has loomed over vampires for ages. This is just one historical "close call."

In 1610, Countess Elizabeth Báthory, a Hungarian of nobility, was caught and tried on charges that she'd killed over six hundred young girls, in the belief that bathing in their blood could keep her young. Báthory was not an actual vampire. She never actually drank blood but was nonetheless suspected of being a vampire by the media.

All the vampires in Hungary shared in the fortuitousness of the Báthory story, as it deflected interest from what could have resulted in a devastating investigation or revelation.

A careless vampire operating in the area had gone on a feeding rampage. By disregarding all normal rules of decorum and culling an excessive number of victims, he'd put himself and all vampires in jeopardy of media scrutiny and possible total exposure.

SLOVACĂ SANTINELĂ
AMERICANESC PRODUCĂTOR ALAN DURBIN TREI ORB DOARECII ADUCE LA SCENĂ MARE.
Sânge Bathory: Nobil femeie asta a fost omorâDi 600 Dărânesc Girls Pur Di simplu fantastic– Sau e un vampir?
ARMATA POLONEZI AJUNGE NOU CIZME

Blood Báthory: Was noblewoman who killed 600 peasant girls simply fanciful—or is she a vampire?

ZECI DE CITY REZIDENAILOR PLÂNGÂNDU-A GÂTULUI DE RANI, SIND RECE TOT ORA: AUTORITATILE MEDICALE CONSILIEREA SÂNGERARE.
Etiam eu justo nec nunc rutrum feugiat. Curabitur placerat. Vivamus quam purus, ad-

Dozens of city residents complaining of neck sores, being cold all the time: Medical authorities advise bloodletting

SOME PRACTICAL TIPS FOR AVOIDING THE MEDIA

- Scout all new feeding locales for security cameras to ensure that you aren't recorded engaging in vampiric activity.
- If in an urban environment with a sizable human celebrity population, direct those possessing recording devices away from where you wish to feed by reporting a celebrity sighting several blocks away. Choose a celebrity of note so that humans don't just roll their eyes.
- Stay away from burning buildings, multiple-car pileups, and trapped-miner rescue operations. Also avoid the homeless on Thanksgiving Day.
- Never allow yourself to be videotaped having sex with a human.

If the media proves inescapable, there are ways to effectively counter most forms of analog and digital recording.

COUNTERING AN ATTEMPT TO CAPTURE YOUR IMAGE

- Handheld 110,000-lumen flash devices are vampire-safe and can be used to distort a picture as it is being taken, in addition to blinding those responsible.

> **MILES SAYS:**
> Always check that your batteries are still good. Take it from a vampire who knows—there's nothing more infuriating than a flash that doesn't go off because the batteries are dead.

- A neodymium magnet* has the strength to erase memory storage.

> **MILES SAYS:**
> Be careful with neodymium magnets. I once wore one on a necklace and had a house key stuck to the back of my neck for a month before I noticed.

- Smoke grenades emit a dense cloud that allows you plenty of time and cover to disable security cameras undetected.

> **MILES SAYS:**
> I always go with black smoke, but they come in a rainbow of colors.

On occasion, your caution and preventative measures may not be enough. Always have a plan ready in case you have to deal with a crisis.

WHAT TO DO IF COMPROMISED BY A MEMBER OF THE MEDIA

1. Immediately incapacitate the human responsible.
2. Seize all devices and determine whether the situation has been contained.

---

*A neodymium magnet is the strongest type of permanent magnet. Each one has a coercivity of about 10,000–12,000 oersteds.

3. Where possible, use the device to send a follow-up message conveying that the entire thing was a joke or a hoax.
4. Transport the human to your lair.
5. Melt down the devices and use your powers of suggestion to convince him that he alone was responsible for the entire episode. Then return him to humanity.

21

GETTING IN: INVITE-ONLY BUILDINGS

THE FIRST TIME you try to enter an **invite-only building** without an invitation, you'll be in for one of the oddest sensations you will ever experience. You confidently saunter up the walkway with ease, but as soon as you hit the door's threshold, your body feels numb and detached, like an arm that has been slept on funny all night. The entrance is right there, yet you utterly lack the ability to pass through it.

The new vampire is easily frustrated by this phenomenon and often attempts to skirt the problem by limiting feeding to public spaces, but killing in these areas can needlessly raise your profile. In addition, an invite-only building may be your only escape from a dangerous situation. If the sun is rising and there is but a lone country home in the distance, without a plan to gain access you could find yourself in great peril.

TYPES OF INVITE-ONLY BUILDINGS

While it's not clear why vampires need permission to enter some places, it is clear which buildings require permission and which do not. Thanks to the work of the Karzack Project (see Appendix IV: Online Resources), vampires now have access to an ever-expanding database of entry instructions for countless locations. The following buildings represent a variety of permission categories, including **general-access areas** and **hybrid structures** that include both public and invite-only areas; it should be noted, however, that many exceptions exist.

BUILDING TYPE	EXAMPLE	ENTRY REQUIREMENTS
Single-family home	The Lutterman home, Pasadena, California	Verbal invitation from a resident.
Apartment building	The Woodmere Building, Chicago, Illinois	No invitation needed for lobby access. Doorman permission required to enter elevators to residential floors.
Convenience store	CVS No. 1593, Scranton, Pennsylvania	General access; bathroom requires key.
Dance club	HoT MeSS, New York, New York	$50 cover for males, $250 for table service; must hypnotize bouncer.
Deli/Restaurant	Benny's, Tamarac, Florida	General access, but for a table, vampires must be seated by hostess.
Shopping mall	The Highland Commons, Scottsdale, Arizona	General access.
Museum	The Milwaukee Art Museum, Milwaukee, Wisconsin	$14 admission, $12 for seniors and vampires who appear to be seniors, $10 for students (with ID), free for members.

BUILDING TYPE	EXAMPLE	ENTRY REQUIREMENTS
Corporate office	Law offices of Haggard, Stook, Goldberg, James & Delman, Vicksburg, Mississippi	Vampires must check in with Valerie at the front desk. Permission from a temp receptionist is invalid.
Movie studio lot	Universal Studios, Burbank, California	Vampire can only enter with a drive-on at Gate 2, off Lankershim Boulevard and James Stewart Avenue. Security provides map and directions to lot offices.
Commune	The Rainbow Haven, Chilamate, Costa Rica	All are welcome.

ENTRY RHETORIC

Standing at the entrance of an invite-only building, a vampire will find that his physical advantages are useless. A would-be victim could be mere inches away, but no amount of speed or muscle can overcome that domestic barrier. The vampire at the gates must use an arsenal of words. Rhetorical tactics are the only way to gain entry.

ASK NICELY

Sometimes the best solution is the simplest one. If you want to gain home access, try asking politely for permission. A little common courtesy goes a long way.

THE SOCRATIC DIALOGUE

Posing incessant questions is a cogent method for getting into a home. A victim will eventually get sick of standing in a doorway answering your queries and invite you in just so she can sit down. The trick of the Socratic tactic is to always base your question on the last part of the previous statement.

HUMAN: *You can't come in. I'm going to the gym.*

VAMPIRE: *Do you really think you need to go to the gym?*

HUMAN: *Exercising is good for your health.*

VAMPIRE: *Would you agree that health is worthless if you are not happy?*

HUMAN: *Sure. I suppose that makes sen—*

VAMPIRE: *And does exercising make you happy?*

HUMAN: *No.*

VAMPIRE: *Do you want me to come in and provide you with happiness?*

HUMAN: *I'll put a teakettle on the stove. Come on in.*

And just like that you're on her neck.

CREATE A CRISIS

One of the fastest ways to get into an invite-only home is to feign panic and create an immediate sense of urgency.* Alarmist behavior often trumps the wisdom of letting in a stranger. A touch of theatricality can aid your endeavor. A bloodied bandage on the head, a knife sticking out of the rib cage, a frantically wagged missing-child flyer—any of these great props can add an air of legitimacy to your pleas for personal assistance. When creating a crisis, the opening line is of the utmost importance.

Opening Line Sampler:

"Help! I'm going into anaphylactic shock!"

"Open the door! I need to call the prison and stop an execution!"†

"Oh my God, let me in! There's a vampire after me!"

---

*When using the create-a-crisis method, be aware of cultural and regional norms. What constitutes an emergency situation in one country could be status quo in another.
†When using this opening line, wear a suit and comb your hair like a governor.

The Professional House Call Method

Do not use this method. It is the first instinct of every vampire to don some ridiculous costume and pretend to be a vacuum salesman, an Amnesty International volunteer, or a Zoroastrian proselytizer. These are characters whose job it is to get inside homes, so it's understandable that a new vampire would use their identities as cover.* Think back, however, to when you were a human. When, if ever, did you let one of these door-to-door pitchmen into your home? Hopefully the answer is never; thus there is no reason to believe that you would have any more success than they did. This strategy is further hobbled by the fact that you'll be approaching many homes in the middle of the night, when home owners are exponentially less likely to invite a roaming salesperson inside. Unless you're a child vampire selling Girl Scout cookies or gift-wrapping paper for a school drive, you will not successfully invade any domicile using the professional house call tactic.

*One near success was documented in Topeka, Kansas, in 1992. A local coven posed as a group of sweepstakes prize deliverers and showed up at a home in the dead of night with balloons and an oversized novelty check. Unfortunately, they forgot to bring a television camera and the home owners refused to believe they'd won since, in the words of one resident, "It'd be on TV if it were real."

SOCIETY AND CULTURE

22

FINDING AND APPROACHING OTHER VAMPIRES

AFTER SPENDING COUNTLESS YEARS avoiding detection, most vampires learn to blend like chameleons among the warm. The unfortunate by-product of this anonymity is that they also become extremely difficult for other vampires to locate.

There is no easy, surefire way to track down another of your kind. Intervampiric telepathy is not in your arsenal of powers, and since the careful and cultured vampire knows to always wear enclosed shoes, he leaves no viscous trails to his lair.

When you want to connect with another vampire, the search can be fruitless and frustrating if you don't know where and how to look. You may have already tried seeking out other vampires by stalking graveyard catacombs but have nothing to show for it but a pair of dirty pants and a keepsake femur. The newly turned are often under the false impression that they can find an associate among the crumbling remains of the truly dead, despite the fact that there's no reason a vampire would hang out in such a trite place where there's nothing to do.

> **MILES SAYS:**
> After a few negative encounters, I eventually figured out where the types of vampires I'm interested in spend their time—community college night classes, fashion shows, midnight movies—and the locations I should actively avoid—improv shows, raves, and interstate rest stops.

In reality, vampires are probably present just about everywhere you go. It's possible that you strolled right past a kindred creature at the bowling alley or were behind one in line to buy scratch-offs without realizing it. If you while away the hours in twenty-four-hour gyms watching humans get red in the face, there's no reason to think another of your kind doesn't enjoy doing the same. Only a limited number of places are open all night, so look around.

SIGNS THAT A VAMPIRE IS NEAR

When you're looking for another vampire, it is often easier to tell where he has been, rather than where he currently is.

Vampire glyphs are the surest way to know that someone is reaching out and trying to communicate with others in his midst. These are universally understood marks that vampires leave for one another to provide tips about the people and establishments in a local area. (See Appendix II: Glyph Guide.) A glyph can be jotted anywhere, from a doorjamb to the fender of a taco truck. Since no vampire wants to be caught making one, many are low to the ground, often scrawled quickly while pretending to tie a shoelace or pick up a lucky penny. If you'd like to leave your own marks in the hope that a vampire might find you, work with any type of perma-

> ### A Word on Etiquette
>
> Stumbling upon a vampire in the act of feeding provides you with an immediate positive ID, but it is considered a firm social taboo to introduce yourself at that time. Make a note of his physical characteristics and seek him out another night.

nent ink and avoid blood, which is not only risky but also water-soluble.

APPROACHING A SUSPECTED VAMPIRE

Now that you have an idea about where to look, the next hurdle is picking a vampire out of a crowd. Someone with otherworldly, luminous skin may arouse your suspicions, but before you foolishly reveal yourself to a human who just had a pricey facial, know that there is one reliable test to determine if he is what you think he is. Stare. Humans blink ten to fifteen times every minute, on average, but if determined can sometimes avoid blinking for up to three minutes. Vampires have no need to blink and do so only when directly interacting with a human. Lock your suspect's gaze and time it. If he crosses that three-minute threshold without blinking, you have found another vampire.

THE VAMPIRE'S REACTION

Once you have confirmed his true nature, it's up to the other vampire to make the next move. By staring, you have extended an invitation; it's his option to accept or decline. You will know whether or not he is interested in an introduction by one of two responses.

Flashing a fang is a friendly gesture similar to a human wink. It acknowledges a willingness to fraternize, and future contact is promised.

A stare not followed by the flash of a fang indicates that he has no interest in taking things any further. If he should instead crush a rock in his hand, you are dealing with a territorial and extremely antisocial vampire. It is best to keep your distance.

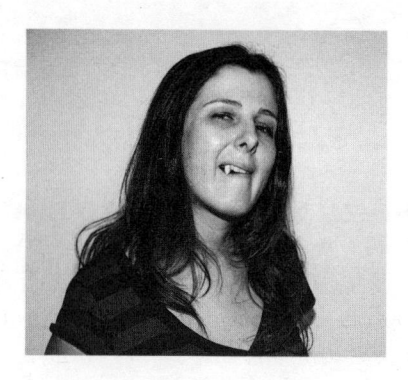

23

COVENS

COVENS* ARE THE IMMEDIATE social units in the larger vampire community. They are close-knit family-like groups that stay together for centuries. You may be reluctant to join a coven because of your previous experiences with human families. While this is understandable, you should recognize that covens are not some slapdash hodgepodge of genetic traits. They are better than families. They have shared purposes, goals, and aspirations, and the vampires in them come together by choice. Think of them as a fraternity everybody wants to pledge, but without sweatshirts and with slightly more bloodshed. The type of coven you enter should reflect your sensibilities, skills, and desires. Just as important, you must have the right look. Don't take it personally if you appear to be eighty-four years old and thus are not admitted into a children's coven. Just because you don't look the part, it doesn't mean you're any less of a vampire.

---

*Also called *coteries* in South America, *clans* in Europe and Australia, *tribes* in Asia, and *nests* in Africa.

COVEN CLASSIFICATIONS

MAINSTREAM COVENS

Mainstream covens are human family doppelgängers, interacting with their living counterparts in suburbs and townships. "Mainstream" refers to their resemblance to the most common human form of grouping, but this coven type is actually exceedingly rare. Mainstream covens are extremely unstable and ineffective. Suburban living requires taking part in neighborly activities such as backyard barbecues, garage sales, and trash-can Thursdays—all of which would put you squarely in the deadly rays of the sun. To live as a mainstream coven, you will always have to have excuses at the ready for why you never participate in these activities, but these excuses could turn your members into the outcasts of the block; by attempting to fit in, you will ultimately stand out.

Making these covens all the more tenuous, the human family dynamic is often at direct odds with the vampire hierarchy; this can lead to confusing and detrimental consequences. If, for example, the teenage-looking vampire of the mainstream coven is 460 years

The Smithberg Coven of Reston, Virginia

old and the middle-age-looking vampire of the coven is only 275 years old, the elder vampire will have to subvert his own authority in public.* This scenario can occur only so many times before the unruly 275-year-old adolescent starts to honestly believe that he is in charge. These intra-coven feuds never end peacefully.

CORPORATE COVENS

The *corporate coven* takes the worst parts of humanity—greed, insurmountable hierarchies, strict dress codes—and utilizes them in a structure that makes for both a good cover in the mortal world and an effective vampire organization. The corporate structure allows vampires to lure human clients and business associates to conference rooms for productive dinner meetings, and the sight of office lights on at all hours of the night will instill confidence in the company work ethic, rather than raise suspicions that you're running a streamlined bloodletting operation. Another strong feature of the corporate coven is the potential for expansion. A mainstream coven that adds a new member every week will be seen as freakish, whereas a corporate coven that adds a new member every week is a booming business ripe for investment.

The TP Rockwell Investment Bank Coven, New York, New York

---

*The scenario is technically referred to as **inverse hierarchical sublimation**.

When starting a corporate coven, hire a crackerjack accounting firm to keep the books clean, as a preventative measure. The last thing a corporate coven needs is some state attorney general who's looking to make a name for himself by going after the company.*

ARISTOCRATIC AND APARTMENT CO-OP COVENS

Typically, *aristocratic covens* are loath to take on the newly turned because there is a high level of maturity and financial means expected among members. The original European aristocratic covens were large landowning dynastic organizations that emulated the wealthy human families of the day and lived off the blood of peasants and nobles alike. After moving westward to America, they reduced their sizes; developed a taste for canal diggers, newsies, and Irish immigrants; and emblazoned their names on buildings and plazas throughout Manhattan. Today, aristocratic covens are rarely larger than 150 members, all of whom live under a single, lavish

The Beauregard Coven, London, England

---

*Although ordinarily the killing of a high-profile governmental figure would be inadvisable, a coven could theoretically kill a state attorney general and not be suspected if there is adequate Mafia activity in the region.

roof of what's called a co-op apartment building. The life is easy—operas, gallery openings, black-tie orgies—but, inevitably, members become bored with the existence. Sipping on the same old blood of human tenant applicants always tastes of sad desperation, even if it is held in a crystalline Swarovski goblet.

DRIFTER COVENS

What a *drifter coven* lacks in luxury it makes up for in variety. Every night a different city, every meal a different kind of human. For those vampires who want to live off the grid, traditional drifter covens are ideal. Keep the size of the coven small, as sleeping in an RV can be a somewhat cramped affair, and get blackout treatments on your camper windows. Regularly crossing time zones on the road can wreak havoc on your internal clock, and you don't want to be caught driving during an earlier-than-expected sunrise.

CHILDREN'S COVENS

Kid vampires simply don't fit into most covens. Obviously, they work well in mainstream covens, but very few elder-but-baby-faced vampires want to live in such a low-class situation. Child labor laws prevent them from joining corporate covens, co-op covens don't allow them unless they're accompanied by an older-looking vampire, and drifter-coven children always run the risk of being dragged away by a crusading member of child and family services. In light of these difficulties, *children's covens* were formed as a welcoming environment for the cherubic among us. Boarding schools and orphanages in particular provide excellent covers* for children's covens, although it is important to recruit adult slaves to add to the authenticity of the operation.

---

*Teen vampires must take care to adorn their flawless vampiric skin with acne blemishes in order to keep up appearances. This provides personal cover to complement the structural cover of the children's coven.

The Bishop Academy Coven, Tewksbury, Massachusetts

STUDY-ABROAD COVENS

If you're a twenty-something vampire who has an adventurous streak, a collection of baseball hats and hoodies, and a taste for doe-eyed European ladies and wandering college graduates, consider joining a *study-abroad coven*. It's important to settle each year in a

The University of Tempe Study-Abroad Coven, Gstaad, Switzerland

new place where you don't know the language. Humans will be able to sense your ignorance of the surroundings, and that cluelessness will draw them to your fangs. Ingenues will flock to your coven for the rare chance to sleep with a foreigner, and opportunistic thieves will want to get close in order to rob you.

"VAMPIRE" COVENS

Pretending to be a group of humans who think they're vampires might be the best cover for a group of vampires who don't want to be bothered by humans. Most vampires find it undignified to don capes, white makeup, and fake fangs, but it is a superb costume to make the majority of humans want to stay far, far away from you.

The Billings-Area "Vampire" Coven, Billings, Montana

24

FEUDS

IT IS AN unpleasant fact of vampire existence, but from time to time, you may find yourself at cross-purposes with another vampire. Vampires can be just as vengeful, plotting, proud, jealous, vain, vindictive, power mad, and cruel as their human counterparts.

A vampire's anger can fester and grow for literally hundreds of years. Over time, repeated abuses or infractions add fuel to a fire that finally manifests as a devastating, uncontrollable physical rage so encompassing that a vampire is incapable of rational judgment or discretion.

More serious grievances that go unresolved can create long-standing animosities between vampires that lead to public exposure, serious injury, or even death. That's why vampires strive to avoid confrontation whenever possible. It's also why conflict resolution is so important to the vampire community.

There are any number of reasons why vampires feud: simple personality conflicts, squabbles over territory, and domestic or romantic quarrels within covens are all common catalysts. Often, the vampire who was socially maladjusted in his previous life continues to have difficulty in his new one.

Thankfully, these types of petty arguments, minor skirmishes, and misunderstandings greatly outnumber the epic, full-scale wars, and can usually be resolved peaceably.

Many vampires find resolution by engaging one another in constructive dialogue, often in a neutral setting. They'll proceed to discuss the issue until they are capable of reaching an agreement. If they cannot do that, they will simply agree to disagree, shake hands, and go on their separate ways.

When a conflict proves intractable, however, it moves into a formal arbitration.

ARBITRATION

Vampires long ago realized that immortals must have peaceful means through which to solve their conflicts, and the formal

> **MILES SAYS:**
> As a vampire of somewhat reliable reputation, I've been called on many times to arbitrate. Most of the cases were petty and forgettable, but a rare few challenged and delighted me. In 1609, I heard the pleas of the Vampires Captain Phillip Nielsen and Peter Goodwich, two Britons who successfully operated a shipping concern. When Nielsen killed several mutinous crew members rather than deal with their grievances, morale aboard the ship—and with it, productivity and profit—sank to new lows. Goodwich felt cheated, and wanted Nielsen disciplined. As someone prone to seeking simple solutions for complicated situations, I certainly sympathized with Nielsen, but he had clearly been in the wrong.
>
> Yet the business had previously been so successful that I didn't wish to destroy the union. I ruled that Captain Nielsen formally apologize to Goodwich in writing and that Goodwich be given an honorary title of his own, as well as a hat with a medallion pinned to it. In my experience, it's the little things that bring about successful mediations. Everyone was pleased, and the two continued their very successful venture for several hundred more years.

process of arbitration dates back thousands of years. Conflicts that occur within a coven are arbitrated by the head of that coven.

When two vampires from separate covens have a matter they wish settled, or if one or more of the parties is unaffiliated with a coven, a third, neutral party of high standing is brought in to settle the conflict.

In the extremely unlikely event that an impartial, unrelated third party cannot be found, a local **High Council** representative steps in to arbitrate and mediate the conflict.

If arbitration is unsuccessful or if a personal conflict escalates, feuding vampires have two remaining options.

THE HIGH COUNCIL OF VAMPIRES

The High Council was formally convened in A.D. 896 near what is now Budapest, after a full-scale war between Moravian and Magyar vampires erupted and wiped out nearly a quarter of the population in the region.* The council successfully worked to defuse the conflict, address remaining grievances, and ultimately reconcile the two groups. The High Council still formally mediates conflicts between warring vampires that cannot be resolved by other means.

Although individual vampires are free to petition the High Council with their complaints, the council hears only about twenty personal-grievance cases every one hundred years, and chooses them based on their intrinsic value to vampirekind. No enforcement body exists to ensure that the involved parties abide by the ruling, and the council's resolutions are not binding. However, its judgment is well respected and is generally regarded as the final word on a matter.

The vast majority of personal conflicts do not merit a hearing by

---

*The vampire conflict was concurrent with a human conflict in which the Magyars ultimately brought about the disintegration of the Great Moravian Empire. Unlike the humans, the vampires were fighting not over territory but over the Moravians' absurd notion that all of vampirekind should adopt the Moravian Czechoslovakian dialect as its official tongue.

the council, but they still require resolution. If all attempts to resolve a conflict peaceably have been made in good faith and have failed, the conflict will be resolved by the unsavory, yet sometimes necessary means of violent engagement.

BATTLING ANOTHER VAMPIRE

Because vampires have the ability to heal rapidly, it is unlikely that one side in a fight will capitulate and declare the other a winner. Very rarely does a confrontation result in anything less than death for one of the participants. Always fight with that point in mind. Once the battle begins, there is but one fundamental imperative: conclude it quickly. In close-quarters combat with a vampire, the targets are principally the head and heart regions.

An arranged duel affords the luxury of time to prepare. Use any advance knowledge of the location and time of the duel to set a trap for your opponent. Always test any system in advance to ensure that it will function properly to avoid embarrassment.

> **MILES SAYS:**
> I have been in only a handful of fights with other vampires over the entire span of my existence, and they all ended in an instant. There weren't any long, protracted sequences of trading punches back and forth, interspersed with chatty exchanges by both parties. No wrestling around and crashing through skylights or walls. No running across the room at each other before leaping into the air for a dazzling aerial duel replete with judo throws. No tackle moves where the floor got peeled up because the force of the collision was so intense. No elaborate swordplay that contained elements of fencing. And never was there any slow motion. No, my fights ended immediately because I punched a silver spike concealed between the fingers of my gloved hand through the heart of my opponent as we were readying to begin. He never knew what hit him. If a fight can't be avoided, I don't wait for a formal start to the proceedings; it's over before it begins.

IMPALE HIM

Impaling is simple, but tried and true. If you do it right, an opponent will struggle to get free for only a few moments before realizing he's finished.

Preparation:
- A minimum of ten stakes with very sharp ends, at least three feet in length.

Execution:
- Stick as many of the stakes as you can in a room so that they protrude from the walls or doors. Force the vampire onto one of the spikes. Make sure adequate force is applied so that he is completely impaled.

CRUSH HIM WITH A CAR

This trap requires a specific location, but dropping a car on your adversary sends you on your way.

Preparation:
- Find a junkyard with a magnetic crane.

Execution:
- Pick up a car with the magnetic crane.
- While being followed by your opponent, leave a trail of seeds from the junkyard's entrance to under the suspended car. (Be careful not to look at the seeds as you are dropping them. Consult chapter 3, "Weaknesses," for more information.)
- Climb into the crane.
- Wait as the vampire follows the seed trail to its end.
- Drop the car.

BURN HIM

The sun is the most effective and easiest way to burn up a vampire, but getting one into the light is not easy. Obfuscation and trickery,

SOCIETY AND CULTURE

The Curtains at Dawn Trap

such as that employed in the Curtains at Dawn Trap, is integral to any successful effort.

Preparation:
- Find a room at least a hundred feet long with a large window on its east-facing wall.
- Install a trapdoor leading to a safe area below the floor approximately twenty-two feet from the window.
- Hang a minimum of six black curtains so that they span the entire width of the room and are approximately fifteen feet apart.

Execution:
- Stipulate that the duel must take place just before dawn. Begin insulting the other vampire upon arrival, then flee and make sure he gives chase. Keep him close, but not too close.
- Lead him into the curtain room. Pass through all the curtains except the last, continuing to goad him all the while.
- Slip down the trapdoor undetected. Sweep up his ashes the next night.

25

VAMPIRE DIVERSITY

IF YOU WERE ONCE a middle-class Korean mechanic or an Afro-Cuban busker, the transformation wasn't just a shock; it was probably also deeply puzzling. It's certain you were familiar with the human view of what a stereotypical vampire looks like and knew it had nothing in common with you.

All newly turned vampires are brimming with questions, but for those who were not white males of some means, the first question often isn't "Why the hell am I a *vampire*?" but "Why the hell am *I* a vampire?"

It is true that for centuries the vampire ranks were dominated by Eastern Europeans who maintained an insular bloodline, as was the practice when they were humans. They occasionally embraced new members from neighboring villages, but only out of necessity when some fresh blood was needed for the increasingly inbred stream. These recruits were chosen for no other reason than their ability to blend within the established clan.

Eventually, a few vampires struck out to see the world and developed an appreciation of and fondness for the cultures they visited.

MILES SAYS:

When I was with Zlatan, we'd occasionally take excursions to exotic locales. On one such visit to Morocco we were unexpectedly approached during a feeding by Mohammed, a local ethnic vampire who was thrilled to finally meet others of his kind. Zlatan was irritated by the whole thing, but it was the first time I'd even known that a non-European vampire existed, and I was excited. Mohammed had been turned a few years earlier by a visiting Frenchman who then abruptly split town, and he was still struggling with some of the basics. As I tried to give him some pointers, we soon figured out that with my tourist looks and his knowledge of the area we could band together to form a two-vampire killing machine. That outrageous Moroccan and I had an amazing month slaughtering Berbers together, and the experience really opened my eyes.

Some of them even chose to secretly turn the new friends they made, returning home with a much more progressive view of what makes a good vampire candidate.

As vampires began to migrate to all corners of the globe, it became obvious that the old tradition was impossible to sustain, and eventually vampires came to grips with how backward and ridiculous such an exclusionary policy had been all along. The diversified ranks broadened feeding opportunities, allowed access to previously inaccessible culling grounds, and made it much more difficult for humans to detect the vampires among them.

When new recruits are chosen solely for their potential to make excellent vampires, and not for their ability to match portraits hang-

We're all in this together, forever!

ing in the ruling families' lairs, the community is made that much stronger.

Your former racial identity no longer has any bearing on your new existence except as a cosmetic benefit when hunting or interacting with the warm. You no longer have a prefix. You are simply a vampire.

26

SOCIAL RESPONSIBILITY

THE CONCEPT OF SOCIAL RESPONSIBILITY is best expressed by the timeless vampire adage "To act in self-preservation is to act in the best interests of all."

If a vampire puts himself at risk, he exposes every vampire to the

> **MILES SAYS:**
> I went through a period early on when I behaved as if living forever was a foregone conclusion and no harm could befall me. I fed too much. I fed in the same areas. I leapt from rooftop to rooftop in the full moon's light. Luckily, I still had Zlatan as a mentor. Grabbing me by the ear he said, "You think those powers are always going to bail you out? What if you're discovered when you're out there acting like nothing can hurt you and it comes back on me? Do you think I want to get staked because you fed on the burgher's daughter?" It took Zlatan ripping off my ear to make me take vampire social responsibility seriously. I patiently waited for the ear to reattach and approached each night thereafter with a different attitude.

same. A vampire must sustain and protect himself above all else. If another vampire infringes on or impedes your ability to stay secure or feed, that is reckless, and you have the right of redress.

Your future is not independent of humanity's. The more stable the human population, the more secure your blood supply. Sometimes being socially responsible means being a shepherd if you can because self-preservation is not always a human strong suit.

As a vampire, you now transcend the mortal and moral constraints of humans, but you still have a responsibility to vampirekind. Focusing entirely on preserving your own well-being will help ensure that other vampires will always have the chance to do the same.

Selected Historical Examples of Socially Responsible Behavior

Socially responsible vampires have a long record of emphasizing both their own security and the sustainability of the human population.

- At some personal risk, the Aegean vampire Aella used his considerable persuasive talents to foster the human transition from the Bronze Age to the Iron Age and ensured that a Silver Age was not even considered.
- The Roman vampire Basilius decided that rather than risking a loss of anonymity by switching to his preferred color, black, he would continue to wear a white tunic like the human patrician population.
- The vampire Petraracha, who considered himself a vampire first and a scholar second, refrained from correcting his Renaissance-era colleagues when they concluded that the existence of vampires was superstitious folly.
- Rather than decimating the few settlers who survived the voyage to Jamestown, the accompanying vampire colonist Thevenin subsisted on mosquitoes until additional colonialists arrived.
- When bringing vampirism to Japan, the vampire Jesturn resisted even tasting a drop of samurai blood, for fear that he would be tempted to turn one and potentially create an unstoppable warrior class.
- The vampire Ibn invented, promoted, and popularized the use of a disposable fang covering that allowed the taking of blood by vampires but helped minimize the collateral spread of the HIV virus among the African human population.

WORDS TO LIVE FOREVER BY: To become socially responsible, focus on the Four B's, the Core Vampire Values:

Be aware of safety and security.
Be for yourself.
Be proud of your history.
Be ready to live forever.

27

RELOCATING

IN THE ABSENCE of a stable mentor, you are strongly urged to relocate shortly after the transformation. Virtually all aspects of vampire existence are incompatible with your former identity.

Your old life is now behind you and a new one lies in front; go forward unencumbered. Becoming a vampire is difficult enough; don't needlessly carry past burdens. If you weren't happy as a human, this is an opportunity for the freshest of starts.

WHERE TO GO

Carefully choose both the geographic area and the actual site where you'll reside as a vampire. Begin your search by keeping in mind that no one place provides all things. There is no vampire Shangri-la. Gather as much information as possible and base your decision on the practical and personal benefits each destination offers.

An alternative way to research a locale you are interested in with-

> **MILES SAYS:**
> I once settled in the unlikeliest of places: Columbus, Ohio. The city held an allure because it satisfied my practical needs and yet offered an unfamiliar midwestern sensibility. My research had also revealed that it was home to a surprisingly good art museum. There I met and befriended Wendell. Wendell had lived his entire human life in Columbus prior to becoming a vampire. He was freshly turned and ready to move on but absolutely certain that California was the only place for him. "This place sucks! Good riddance. I'm heading to California, where I heard there's tons of stuff going on all the time and everybody's cool," Wendell would say. Despite my admonitions not to rely on preconceptions he'd held as a human, Wendell moved to Los Angeles without any further research, only to call me back in Columbus a short time later. "Man, everyone here is just out for themselves," he said, disappointed. Wendell then understood that he needed to be far less impulsive about relocating, and I gave him pointers on how to investigate a new area. Last I heard he was still finding the River Walk and life in San Antonio "the best."

out actually visiting is to feed on a few humans who live there. Much about a place is revealed by the blood of its inhabitants. Diet, the presence of carcinogens, and the levels of mood-stabilizing drugs will sometimes reveal more than any other research. Airports provide a representative sample of the human population from other places. Bus stations do not.

CHOOSING A LAIR

After settling on where to go, you'll need to find a lair. A lair serves as a secret retreat that both protects a vampire's identity and houses his coffin. The primary consideration when choosing a lair should be security.

Depending on your financial situation, a lair can take the form of many dwellings: a house, condo, apartment, or manor. Do not overextend yourself financially for a lavish lair. Paying for it will preoccupy you unnecessarily. Until you find an ideal one, consider taking up residence in a temporary lair. (For more information see Appendix III: Temporary Lairs.)

A permanent lair can be found by seeking out a single elderly home owner who has lost her spouse and is happy just to have someone to talk with. Often neither suggestion nor mind control is necessary to bend such a person to a vampire's will. But take care to learn about the situation before attempting to seize the property. Don't underestimate how angry, enraged, vindictive, and insane the home owner's absentee relatives will become when the estate is settled and they are out of the will. Better to look for someone with no family. Then the only things between you and ownership of the property are a signature and nine pints of blood, which is the easiest thing of all to take.

A final factor to consider is your potential lair's proximity to available blood supplies. Don't put yourself in a situation where long commutes are required for you to feed. You'll begin to resent the amount of work it takes to do the simplest of things each night.

28

SLAVES

WITH THE ADVENT of twenty-four-hour retail, vampires are now able to live much more conveniently than in the past. But despite easy access to many goods, services, and amenities, it is wise to consider acquiring a human **slave.** Slaves are invaluable for completing transactions that require daytime interaction with humans, as well as numerous mundane chores integral to your nightly existence.

While your residual human sensibilities might recoil from the term *slave*, it does not have the same negative connotation in vampire society. These mortals align themselves with vampires willingly and are akin to personal assistants. They are usually not paid, but slaves gain valuable negotiating and organizational skills while in your employ. A vampire should therefore never feel any guilt when mentally manipulating a slave to do his bidding.

There are no directories of humans looking to fill a slave position, but there are several places you can go to locate prospects. Avoid advertising on websites frequented by vampire devotees. Those people will only be interested in learning the secrets of eternal life, and will be full of excuses when it comes to taking out the

> **MILES SAYS:**
> I've created more than one embarrassing and potentially incriminating mess. When I've had a slave on hand, it was always easier to deal with. He would set off for a bottle of bleach, rubber gloves, and a multipack of paper towels, while I secured the scene. Later, I was able to retire confidently, knowing he'd have it all cleaned up by sunset.

trash. Instead, stick to local candidates who are looking for work. "Odd job" flyers hung up in grocery stores are good recruiting resources. Potential hires can also be found sporting sandwich boards or passing out circulars advertising a liquidation sale. Despite the fact that many of these individuals are considered "screwups" by the warm, most are quite eager and in the possession of a varied but useful set of skills, making them ideal slave material.

A slave candidate must be relatively healthy and presentable. Someone with a hacking cough, facial sores, or a habit of wearing novelty T-shirts has limited potential. He should be a nonthreatening presence among other humans, but also the type who wouldn't hesitate to break another man's fingers to complete your tasks. If he's desperate, he'll really appreciate your willingness to take a chance on him, and that can translate into rabid loyalty.

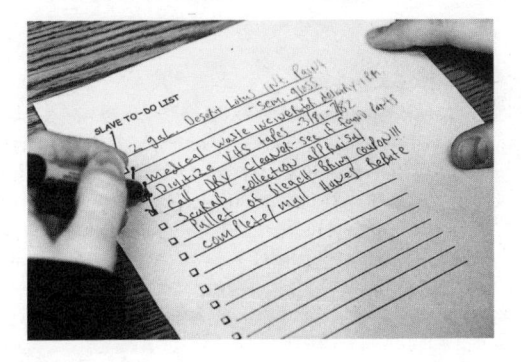

During the evaluation process, be sure he has the ability to maintain direct eye contact and possesses sufficient mental stamina. These qualities are a must for any prospect, since telepathically commanding him to complete tasks requires you to look deeply into his eyes for a period of several minutes, and each time you do so a bit of his sanity will chip away.

Once you've hired a slave, establish firm ground rules for the relationship. Insisting that he refer to you as "Master" is an antiquated practice; he should address you with the standard "Vampire ____." Calling you by your first name only is inappropriately chummy. Make it clear that while he may assist in luring prey, his opinions regarding the selection of the prey will not be considered. Also, by no means should he be under the impression that he has license to redecorate or rearrange your lair.

The most important role a slave fills is that of **lair watchman.** If you've chosen wisely, he will guard your location like Cerberus,* and give his life to defend yours. However, even the most dedicated slave can get bored sitting around all day. Setting up a wireless Internet connection in your lair is a wise investment. Instruct him to monitor blogs for claims of vampire sightings, but there is no need

---

*Cerberus is a mythical multiheaded dog that guards the entrance to the underworld. Dog-napping Cerberus was Hercules' twelfth and final labor.

> **MILES SAYS:**
> Economic downturns are the best time to recruit a new slave. I made my favorite hire in 1980. Paulie was a balloon-game operator who had built a career out of bilking people of their pocket money in exchange for the occasional unicorn mirror. Most humans considered his employment background unseemly, but his hoodwinking skills made him a perfect fit for me. Unfortunately, I was forced to drain him out of desperation when, in 1982, my lair was laid siege by a tenacious group of laid-off autoworkers-cum-vampire hunters. I held on to his last bag of balloons, which I'll include on a memorial scrapbook page when I get around to putting one together.

for a reprimand if he just plays solitaire all day while you slumber. An occupied slave is much less likely to be tempted by an invitation to go party, and therefore it's much less likely that you'll be decapitated with a shovel.

A slave will run all of your daytime errands, which can range from converting large amounts of currency, haggling with a Chinese freighter captain for passage, or attending your favorite designer's afternoon sample sales. These humans don't typically have much in the way of cash flow, so always make sure to provide your slave with gas or train money.

Beyond protection and regular tasks, your slave can also be used for snacking. This can really alleviate your hunting schedule and will increase his devotion as he starts to feel more a part of your vampire world—like he's got some "blood in the game." However, this practice can lead to a more delicate situation. After several years of giving up his neck, your slave may start to pester you to be turned.

It is true that vampires ask a great deal of their slaves, and you may come to feel that you owe him something. However, by that time, he will certainly be well on the road to mental insanity after all the years you've tinkered with his brain. That's not usually the kind of person you want around for eternity. If his mental capacity has been too diminished, do him one last professional kindness by promising you'll turn him at the special place you turn all your new vampires. Then anonymously drop him off at the nearest facility offering long-term psychiatric care.

29

FAMILIARS

THOUGH A SLAVE can be a significant asset to most any vampire, there are some tasks that he or she, as a somewhat ineffectual mortal, simply cannot complete. While slaves can run errands and guard our homes in daylight, **familiars** aid with the tasks of nightly living.

Despite appearances, some of the hounds, snakes, ravens, and bats who assist vampires are not mere animals* but, essentially, demons—malevolent spirits temporarily housed in the body of an animal. These stealth operators can dispatch enemies, go where vampires cannot, see what vampires cannot, and report back on all they encounter. They're capable of handling duties requiring discretion, such as covertly gathering information on a legitimately dangerous slayer or infiltrating a rival coven. Familiars are telepathic, are empathic, and possess myriad unique abilities, such as senses superior to yours or the ability to briefly disappear.

The familiar serves equally well as a trusted confidant, willing

---

*Familiars are not to be confused with the normal, nocturnal animals that vampires can control.

conspirator, loyal mercenary, keen spy, or enthusiastically vicious minion. Their value cannot be underestimated, and any vampire who makes the mistake of treating a familiar like a pet will be sorely remiss.

The services of a familiar do not come cheaply. These creatures work for some form of appeasement. Occasionally, it's mere indulgence: a fondness for a particular food, a well-pampered life, or a human slave to keep it company. More often than not, though, it's quid pro quo: a vampire strikes a bargain with the familiar that puts the vampire in the familiar's service at some point in the future. The familiar is not necessarily obligated to say what he will ask of the vampire. If the vampire doesn't hold up his end of the bargain, the familiar will exact revenge.

However, if you are considering employing a familiar, you are more than likely already in a compromised position, and it is a chance you'll have to take.

CHOOSING YOUR FAMILIAR

Before engaging a familiar, evaluate which animal best suits your needs, but understand the potential ramifications of your selection. You may wish to acquire a bat for its flawless ability to navigate the darkness, but be prepared when it invites the rest of its colony to stay in your lair. A thick black hound will aid you in tracking scents, but its constant howling, barking, and whimpering may inadvertently draw attention. It's important that the familiar you choose has the right qualifications for the task you assign it.

FINDING YOUR FAMILIAR

Stroll the streets just before dawn, when most familiars are out soliciting work. You will probably see many different animals, but only a few of them will be familiars. As a vampire, you are capable of making a supersonic whistling sound that terrifies ordinary animals but does not dismay those possessed by demons. Emitting this sound will help you distinguish common nocturnal creatures, who will flee at your approach, from familiars, who will come running toward you if they are seeking assignment. You should have no trouble enlisting one to aid you.

Common Familiars and Their Demon Forms

BAT: *CHIROPTERA*

OWL: *STRIGIFORMES*

CAT: *FELIS CATUS*

LIFESTYLE

30

KEEPING UP WITH THE TIMES

FASHIONABLE SONGS CHANGE over time. The parachute pants that were once in style now are the mark of a buffoon. The speakeasy where prey was once abundant became a tattoo parlor, which was converted to a bail bondsman's office, which was turned into a cigar bar, which in turn became a yoga studio, yet still, a vampire sits outside and waits for flappers to emerge so he can feed on them.

It is easy for a vampire to remain stuck in the era during which he was turned, but this can lead to problems. The vampire who does not stay current risks becoming a social pariah and a conspicuous target for any vampire hunter or fanatic.

Even if an anachronistic vampire isn't detected, resisting the march of progress has a cumulative effect on one's sense of sanity and well-being. If a vampire doesn't keep up with the times, it's easy for him to begin to feel obsolete, which can in turn lead to reckless hostility. Such a vampire will wind up dead.

There's another, more tangible reason to keep up with the times: human interaction facilitates easier feeding. In order to interact fluidly, you must keep abreast of the latest of everything. As time goes on, trends and technology shift more quickly. Constant vigilance is necessary. Consult multiple media sources on a regular basis in order to stay current. Fall behind for a year and you'll spend two catching up.

SOCIAL MORES

The behavior society tolerates is in a constant state of flux, yet it is probably the easiest thing to stay abreast of. It moves slowly, and dramatic changes are usually precipitated by a great deal of public outrage.* Your nightly interactions with a cross-section of humanity will allow you to gauge what is permissible merely by casual observation. If you see something that seems out of place, follow the lead of those around you. If they appear shocked, then follow suit.

COMMUNICATIONS

Centuries ago, the process of sending messages to one another was static. If you weren't visiting your friend directly, you were sealing an envelope with hot wax and a signet ring and dispatching someone to deliver it. Slowly, then faster, developments took shape. A rudimentary post office was created. The self-sealing envelope saved households a fortune in wax. The telegraph bridged the miles with a series of long and short clicks, soon to be followed by the party-line telephone. Now it's a flurry of activity. The radio, the pager, the mobile phone, and the Internet all arrived in the past one hundred years. Whereas once you could remain in relative isolation, in this age you will be looked on with suspicion if you don't have at least one device that will enable people to contact you anywhere you go.

---

*While this changes with time, it also differs by region. Although the sight of two men in love holding hands might not raise an eyebrow in New York City, more than eyebrows may be raised in the Deep South.

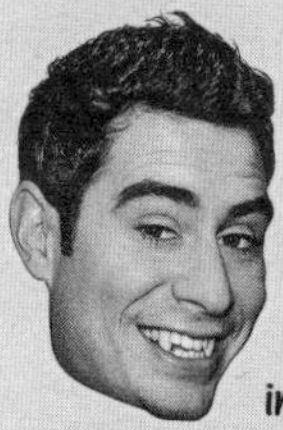

MILES SAYS:

I recently decided that I wanted to contact a friend from the old country. As I could not find his address, I decided that the best way would be via telegraph. I found a Western Union office and proceeded to dictate the contents of my message to the clerk. She simply stood there blankly for several seconds before asking how much money I wanted to send my friend. I tried to explain to her that it wasn't money but just a message that I wanted to convey. She once again asked me how much money I wanted to send him. This went on for some time, until I remembered that the company no longer sends telegrams and is now just a storage space for fluorescent light bulbs and dingy tiles. I chalked my misunderstanding up to hunger, begged her pardon, and left. When I got home, I did what I should have done from the start and looked him up on UndeadConnect.com, my preferred vampire social-networking site.

TRANSPORTATION

It is unlikely that the fundamentals of transportation will evolve anytime soon. You will take either a wheeled or a winged means of conveyance to travel between one locale and another. However, this can all change quite suddenly. Consider, for example, the period between 1820 and 1910. Prior to this, the horse was responsible for nearly all transportation. Suddenly, steam locomotives, automobiles, and airplanes all changed the face of transportation. Will such a quantum shift happen again? Not in the immediate future, but be prepared for the eventuality of space travel and particle transport.

CURRENT EVENTS

At around sixty years of age, small details such as whether or not the country you inhabit is at war tend to blur, no matter how acute your memory. This is why it's good to watch or listen to the news every evening or, at the very least, acquaint yourself with the latest newspaper headlines. Nothing is worse than having a conversation end with suspicion because you started railing about the terrible job President Ford is doing.

MEDIA

Some people say "Information wants to be free," but as time goes on, the means of receiving the information has gotten more expensive. Free town criers gave way to penny newspapers, which gave way to radios, which gave way to televisions, which gave way to computers, each method more expensive than the last. Budget for it. Your investment in the latest media-delivery device is an investment in keeping up with other trends.

TECHNOLOGY

Gadgets proliferate faster and faster every year. It can get overwhelming if you don't keep your eye on the big picture: most technology is for wasting time. Cigarette lighters, video game consoles, digital cameras, MP3 players—none of them can make you happy. It is helpful

> **MILES SAYS:**
> The Vampire Nicolae Cristescu, the oldest vampire I knew in the United States, was a font of wisdom. We met in Philadelphia in the 1920s. Whenever we crossed paths, I eagerly absorbed his lessons about prosperity through caution and discretion. Then, in 1973, he discovered Pong. This simple electronic table tennis simulation game entranced him. Thereafter, whenever I saw him, he would talk about how his score had improved. The last time I saw him, he claimed that he could beat the game. Two weeks later, he was killed by a sunrise when he was playing Pong at a bar. The moral is that technology is just a game. Just let it go.

to be aware of them, and you may even be more attractive to potential prey when you pull out some handheld gizmo or gadget at a bar. In truth, the last great technological advance that helped a vampire in a substantial way was the refrigerator, and something as momentous as a refrigerator comes along only once every hundred years.

SPEECH

It's good to be aware of fluctuations in speech patterns, but don't try to pepper your speech with the argot of youth. No one is fooled by the misuse of slang. Be polite and direct; good manners never go out of fashion. Speak simply and clearly, and punctuate your more important points by breaking someone's arm.

CULTURE

The vampire who vocally laments the death of doo-wop at every opportunity might as well announce to the world that he is a vampire. Likewise, extolling the virtues of the films of Irwin Allen or the novels of James Clavell is also a good way to stand out in the crowd. You live in a time where ignorance of popular culture is scowled upon. Fortunately, there are many magazines that will provide you with photographs of celebrity pregnancies and fashion don'ts. Subscribe to three of these, watch at least two movies a month, and get cable with a premium channel package.

31

STYLE

MANY A NEW VAMPIRE erroneously believes that his personal sense of style goes the way of his mortality. Some spend entire evenings tossing their beloved khakis, football jerseys, and ironic T-shirts into the trash, all the while resigning themselves to a dull eternity of black velvet cloaks and solemn formalwear.

The reality of vampire style, however, is not so black and white. The widely disseminated "classic" look of the vampire is an utter fallacy; it is neither practical, stylish, nor necessary. It's a human construct, and you are not bound by it.

As a vampire, you need to avoid detection—something you may find difficult to do in a full-length silk crepe cape and bolo tie. Today's vampire employs contemporary and classic styles to blend in, rather than stand out. Yet he also needs to catch the eye of potential prey, and to move freely among many different social classes and subcultures.

To do both is a challenge, but with a little effort, a vampire can learn to create looks that strike a balance.

Keep in mind that function and durability are key elements of vampire style. Few garments are designed to withstand the rigors that you will put them through. A healthy coating of Scotchgard, along with reinforcements at the elbows and knees of garments, will protect clothing from excessive wear and the elements. Stain-

> **MILES SAYS:**
> Some vampires have a hard time accepting that their wardrobe might benefit from an update after turning. They ask me, "Am I less of a vampire if I wear sweatpants? Does it matter what I wear?" As a former tailor of exceptional skill, I can assure you that yes, you are, and yes, it does. Your clothing is an extension of you as an individual and as a lethal predator. Tacky and poorly clad vampires embarrass those of us who have an innate understanding of how to look good anytime, anywhere. Also, they are ugly to look at.
>
> Over the years, every vampire will amass a lifetime's worth of fashion faux pas—even one as stylish as myself. Some of my more memorable mistakes include Beatle boots, a flirtation with cowboy hats, skinny jeans, the purchase of a powdered wig in 1943, my "Scottish" phase, and a period in the early 1970s where I thought ponchos looked good on men. Going wrong every once in a while is par for the course, but it's not an excuse to stop trying.

resistant fabrics can cut down on laundering and help keep bloodstains from ruining your favorite pastel items.

With those things in mind, let your personal sense of style run free. Don't be afraid to play with a look. Experimenting is fine, as long as it's within reason. Now that you have infinite time to properly develop a style of your own, you'll find fashion to be an amusing diversion.

SIX RULES FOR STYLE

1. *Fashion fades.* Someone with an eternal life should not spend it in the outfit he wore to the Polk inauguration. Be sure to keep your favorite look tailored to suit the times.
2. *Keep it classic.* Contemporary designers who specialize in classic styles will help you achieve a tasteful, subdued look that gains you entrée into any world you wish to be a part of. It's worth it to invest in at least one sophisticated and well-cut designer suit. Humans are inexplicably compelled to trust a man who wears one.

3. *Don't be afraid of the dark.* No matter the occasion, black is always a great choice. It's sleek, sophisticated, a little bit artsy, masks large bloodstains, and suits the living dead beautifully.
4. *Mix it up.* Incorporate your favorite pieces from various periods of your life. Refer to any items you've had for more than thirty years as "vintage." Fashions tend to be cyclical. The rainbow suspenders you enjoyed in the 1980s may well make a bona fide comeback seventy years from now, so hold on to them.
5. *Learn to love leather.* Leather conveys the coolness and toughness that many vampires exude without being too showy. It's durable, looks even better when distressed, and ages extremely well, which is one reason head-to-toe black leather has become a modern vampire classic.
6. *Say no to shorts.* No one will ever take you seriously in half pants.

A Note on Capes

Far from being an integral part of the vampire ensemble, capes are usually inappropriate, melodramatic, and unwieldy. They do little to help protect your identity, tend to be expensive, and will often lead to your being mistaken for a magician.

However, for the pragmatist, they are not without their uses. They can be used to shield oneself from the rising sun, or one's skin from searing flames. They can be tossed over the head of a captive, or flashed to create a diversion if you're being chased. It bears noting that all of these advantages could be accomplished equally well with the wearing of a long wool coat.

If, in spite of this, you still elect to wear a cape, never buy one off the rack. Always have it tailored to suit your frame.

32

ACTING YOUR AGE

A VAMPIRE'S MIND does not stay frozen in time; it continues to accumulate knowledge and experience forever, long after the body stops aging. There is a point when, intellectually and emotionally, vampires are quite different from mortals of seemingly the same age, but are still expected to behave in the same way.

A vampire who appears to be a seventeen-year-old high school student may have amassed a hundred years of intellect and maturity but is supposed to look forward to attending a prom. Eventually the incongruity must be addressed.

Follow the current characteristics and stereotypes humans hold for your age group. There is a view they have of you at the moment, even if you don't share it, but with the right planning now and knowledge of evolving stereotypes, it will always be impossible for humans to tell how old you really are.

MILES SAYS:
I certainly have to fight **Old Soul Syndrome**. I appear to be in my early twenties, and it's become very difficult for me to relate to humans of that age group, who favor idealism over pragmatism. They are often organizing, marching, assembling, and trying to make the world a better place. I've spent nearly five hundred years experiencing the many stops and starts on humanity's path toward a fully enlightened existence that will never come. I've seen it all before, but I have to appear interested and emotionally invested. It's work, but you don't want to slip up. At a rally to stop gentrification, crying out, "The people with the money have the power—you can whine and yell all you want, but it won't ever change a thing, ever!" is not the way to go. If you're in a youthful body like mine, never let your jaded side show.

A SELECTION OF WESTERN STEREOTYPES, BY AGE AND GENDER

RECENTLY RETIRED MALE
INTERESTS: Shaker furniture
LIKES: Genealogy
DISLIKES: Spicy Oriental food
LIFTS BAGS OF SOFTENER SALT: No
COASTERS: Plenty
HAIR: Just combed
SOLAR-POWERED CALCULATOR: Yes
iPOD: No
SUN CITY, AZ: Yes

THIRTY-SOMETHING FEMALE
IN VITRO: Tried, trying again
MARGARITAS TUESDAY NIGHT?: Yep
PERFORMANCE ON STAIRMASTER: Impressive
DAD: Didn't really know him
LIP BALM: All the time
VOLUNTEER WORK: Dog shelter
SEATTLE: Someday
WASHING MACHINE: Front-loading
FAVORITE ADJECTIVE: Amazing

LIFESTYLE

JUVENILE MALE

PIANO: Yes, but hated it
LAST FRIEND SHOVED: Dominic
FAVORITE MOVIE: 300
FAVORITE BOOK: 300
VIDEO GAME IQ: High
PARENTS: Whatever
COAT: Lost it somewhere
TEXT: y
GIRLFRIEND: Shut up

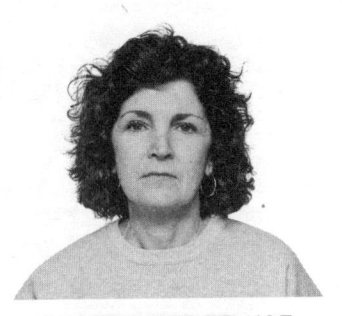

MIDDLE-AGED FEMALE

FIRST DIVORCE: Messy
PATCH: Unsuccessful
VEGAS: Won, just got back
DOG: Poodle
SCENTED CANDLE: Vanilla
BARTENDING EXPERIENCE: Considerable
POWERBALL NUMBER: 15
SOUR-CREAM-AND-ONION CHIP DIP: In fridge
SLIPPERS: On

EARLY-TWENTIES FEMALE

FAVORITE VACATION: Antigua
CREDIT CARD: Has some room
GYM: Quit
EYELASHES: Real
LAST PARTY ATTENDED: Boring
MARSHALL PLAN: Who?
FRIDAY NIGHT: Busy
HEARING: Selective
UNREAD MESSAGES: 54

EARLY-TWENTIES MALE

CAR'S TAILPIPE CIRCUMFERENCE: Huge
MYSPACE: Updated
USE OF "BADASS": Heavy
WEED: Yes
DAD: Less of a dick now
BASS: Fat
COMMUNITY COLLEGE: Under way
NEWPORTS: One left
AFTER BAR: His place

ELDERLY FEMALE

CHURCH CHOIR: Not anymore
DISTANCE OF AVERAGE WALK: One and a half miles
HUSBAND'S OCCUPATION WHEN LIVING: Dentist
FAVORITE CARD GAME: Five hundred
WATER WARMED UP IN MICROWAVE FOR TEA: Never
ATTUNED TO TEMPERATURE: Always
CROSSWORD BOOKS: Stacked in living room
MINT DISH: Full
SUN CITY, AZ: No, sold condo when husband passed away

33

SCRAPBOOKING

INFINITE NEW ADVENTURES, relationships, and kills lie ahead of you, and they will occur within a cultural landscape in constant flux and upheaval. If you don't keep track of them all, special memories can become adrift in history or even fade altogether. Writing in a journal can help you maintain an overall sense of continuity, but to keep the most cherished moments fresh and colorfully alive, nothing beats **scrapbooking.**

The detail and organization required can be extremely time-consuming, but for vampires, that makes scrapbooking an ideal hobby. Not only does it help keep centuries of memories organized in attractively bound displays, but the painstaking, laborious process will fill as many waking hours as you are willing to commit.

To get started, assemble the basic working materials required:

- A scrapbooking album
- Paper in a variety of patterns, colors, and thicknesses*

---

*For preservation purposes, always try to work with acid-free paper.

> **MILES SAYS:**
> I knew that scrapbooking was popular among vampires, but it had never personally interested me. I finally decided to dip my toe in when the fall of communism started making Eastern Europe confusing again. Now I'm totally hooked. For my first project, I chose the 1969 trip I took to visit friends in Bratislava. It was the first time I'd been back since I'd immigrated to the U.S., and so much had changed. When I planned the vacation, the city was in the Czechoslovak Socialist Republic, which the Soviets had recently occupied. But by the time I got there, the country had been divided and *Bratislava* was then the capital of the Slovak Socialist Republic. My friends and I had a fantastic month catching up and feasting on Warsaw Pact troops. I'm glad I finally have an artful reminder of what country those good times actually occurred in. It is currently Slovakia.

- Archival glue
- Hole puncher
- Photo mounts
- Assortment of pens and small paintbrushes
- Craft knife
- Ruler
- Anticoagulants
- Medical slides

When you're ready to begin a project, choose an event to memorialize as well as a contextual theme for the layout, such as springtime, coffins, or the Old West. Next, round up personal artifacts to include on your scrapbook pages. These can include photos, drawings, maps, ticket stubs, stock certificates, or strips of a kill's particularly colorful blouse—just about anything you've kept in your archive. This material doesn't always need to be the focus of the page. Often some of your keepsakes are better used as decorative embellishments. You can use locks of hair you've snipped from victims to create an interesting border fringe or background page texture. Blood-splattered sheet music you've tucked away can make for

F O R E V E R
SLOVAK SOCIALIST REPUBLIC 1969
SCORE!

The Vampire Miles Proctor's maiden scrapbooking project

stylish backgrounds or can be cut up and pasted in a collage-like fashion. For a final special flourish, use any leftovers from the night's meal to inscribe amusing or inspirational quotes to commemorate the event.

Just let your creative side take over as you make your eternity come alive.

34

FINANCES

MANY NEW VAMPIRES wrongly assume that the financial troubles that plagued them during their mortal lives will now somehow disappear. They are shocked to discover that fiscal solvency is more important than ever. Mortals who lose their income have the option of moving in with a boyfriend or girlfriend, a roommate, or, at worst, their aging parents. The vampire has no such safety net, and the same situation for him can have disastrous consequences.

Upon turning, most vampires act as if they have won the lottery. They rush to withdraw the entirety of their meager savings and spend it freely. Most have hardly enough coin to support themselves for a year. How many have enough to live comfortably for two years, let alone an eternity?

Planning for your financial future is a daunting task, but by starting now, you can take steps toward ensuring a financially secure immortality.

PUTTING FIRST THINGS FIRST

If you have substantial savings from your human life, congratulations. Skip ahead to "Creating a 400-Year Plan."

On the other hand, if you were like most mortals, you lived without a financial cushion. You must find some means of generating a new revenue stream immediately.

THEFT: The most obvious occupation for the new vampire is that of the thief. When you bleed a victim, take the opportunity to remove his wallet, car keys, and any valuables he has on him. If you kill the person at his home, take any expensive items on the way out. Selling these items online is an excellent source of income.

ANTIQUES AND COLLECTIBLES: Immortality provides one with a nearly fail-safe source of income: old things. Save everything you can.* Chances are, the things you consider trash today—newspapers, kitschy end tables, cereal boxes, and figurines—will be rare and valuable in the years to come. The vampire who bought a worthless Honus Wagner baseball card for a penny in 1909 is a millionaire today.†

SCAMS: A vampire's lightning-fast reflexes and ability to hypnotize marks make him an ideal flimflam man. Use your speed to work three-card monte games; your long life to help make a Ponzi scheme virtually infallible; and your excellent counting skills at casino blackjack tables.

BOUNTY HUNTER: Bounty hunters receive a monetary award for each fugitive they capture and return to the custody of the authorities. With a naturally intimidating presence, excellent eyes, superior strength, keen tracking skills, and the ability to hypnotize people,

---

*Storage units allow you to conveniently keep all of your acquisitions while maintaining your mobility.
†That vampire is the Vampire Carlos Athanas.

vampires are ideally suited for this type of work. Very occasionally, you have the option of returning a fugitive "dead or alive," making this pursuit both lucrative and nourishing.

Tips for Staying in the System

Many of life's transactions require that you present some proof of identity. When your passport is one hundred thirty years old, it may begin to attract unwanted attention from the authorities.

Establishing and reestablishing new identities will allow you to continue your way of life while deflecting suspicion. It's recommended that you establish a new identity approximately every ten years. Remember:

- A poorly made fake ID can put you needlessly at risk. Always use real documents taken from victims to convincingly create your identity.
- Transferring assets to a slave or assuming his or her identity is a hassle-free method for establishing a new you. Avoid choosing slaves with significant debt, outstanding student loans, or prior bankruptcy filings. A simple credit check during the interview process should tell you all you need to know.
- Establish your identity as a citizen of another country. Several Caribbean nations offer what is known as economic citizenship. Vampires of means can simply fill out the proper forms and pay the requested fee to become a full-fledged citizen of the island of Dominica, with all the rights and privileges that confers.

NEW MEXICO
DRIVER'S LICENSE
License # 283 451 8933
ISSUED 08/15/2008
Date of Birth 05/20/1980
EXPIRES 06/20/2012
Ernesto
Morgensen K
SANTA FE, NM 87508
SEX M
WEIGHT 170
CLASS D
DONOR ♥
HEIGHT 5'09"
EYES BRO
ENDORSEMENTS NONE
RESTRICTIONS NONE

CREATING A 400-YEAR PLAN

A 400-year plan is the first step on your journey to financial freedom. It allows you to make secure provisions for your future but remain flexible, should your wants and needs change as you mature. Break your 400-year plan into centuries or even half centuries in order to keep your eye on the big picture, while maintaining an active list of achievable goals to work toward.

Begin by itemizing your monthly expenses. From there, use your average monthly income to determine how long it will take you to reach those goals. Having a plan is the most important step you can take in ensuring your success.

NAME: Joe J. Vampire   **AGE:** 262

AVERAGE MONTHLY EXPENSE WORKSHEET	COST
MORTGAGE OR RENT	$740/month
OTHER HOME EXPENSES:	$341
Curtains, rods, and accessories	$320
Duct tape	$15
Tinfoil	$6
Food, dining, and groceries	$0
Life insurance	$0
Health insurance	$0
CLOTHING:	$157
Shoes	$40
Socks	$70
Brooches	$12
Dry cleaning, alterations, and stain removal	$35

AVERAGE MONTHLY EXPENSE WORKSHEET	COST
Automobile/Transportation	$35
Slave care	$40
OTHER: Storage Cable Miscellaneous	$149 $20 $79 $50

INVESTMENTS

Vampires tend to be extremely risk-tolerant investors. In your new life, you can and should experiment with the market, or fail to do so at your own peril. Although you can wait out any downward trends in the market, make sure to unload stocks when the time is right. Nineteenth-century vampires who found themselves heavily invested in blubber and spermaceti scoffed at the notion that America's factories might ever run on anything other than whale products. When they refused to change with the times, they were left with little more to show for their strategy than a handful of scrimshaw.

LOOKING TOWARD THE FUTURE

There are more exciting aspects to financial planning than revenue streams and safety nets. You can still pursue your long-held desire to buy a speedboat, build an indoor swimming pool, or purchase a second home in Berne. In fact, your wish list has probably grown to include a luxurious new coffin or security upgrades to your lair.

All these dreams are achievable, even more so now that you literally have forever in which to make them happen. Stay focused. Eventually you'll have the lifestyle you always imagined.

35

COFFINS

CONTRARY TO POPULAR BELIEF, you do not need an actual coffin to get your rest. What is of the utmost import is that you sleep in a lightproof container or vessel that is secured so that it will not pop open of its own volition. A chest freezer, photographic darkroom, washing machine or dryer, refrigerator, or the roomy trunk of a broken-down sedan will all do in a pinch, and one may in fact serve as your sleep vessel for some time after you are turned.

While an appliance you found on the curb may be appealing when the rising sun is bearing down on you, its uncomfortable confines will become intolerable as time wears on.

Sooner or later, there will come a night when you wish to graduate from your poor accommodations to something a little more sophisticated and stable. You will long for a place you can return to at every sunrise, knowing with certainty that you will be able to pass the day there peacefully. In short, you will begin to crave the particular blend of comfort, style, and functionality that only a coffin can provide.

A proper coffin also makes sense from a safety perspective. Mortals are more likely to try opening a stray cooler kept in a backyard

A pilfered body bag can suffice in an emergency.

shed than a strange, ebony-hued coffin kept in a dank, moldy basement. That's just one of the reasons coffins have been favored by vampires for thousands of years. Ironically, humans, who built them for their so-called eternal rest, unwittingly created the perfect vessel in which to spend a good portion of eternal life.

This vampire takes his rest in a wine casket.

MILES SAYS:

Though I was not yet an American, I, too, was devastated when Abraham Lincoln was shot. I had admired the president a great deal, and I followed the news of his assassination. One day the newspaper printed a stunning photograph of the great man's funeral procession, along with a marvelous image of his final resting place. Right then and there, I fell in love.

Lincoln's coffin was nearly six and a half feet of stately black walnut, covered in a wonderful rich ebony fabric, with silver studs all along its sides, arranged cleverly in a shape akin to a shamrock. I'd never seen anything like it, and I felt that the ultimate tribute to this man would be if I could secure myself a similar resting place—although at the time I could not afford one nearly so beautiful or big.

I commissioned the "Little Lincoln" from a talented Romanian coffinmaker named Baboescu. He wasn't a vampire, but he was an unbelievable craftsman, and I was thrilled with his work. I slept in that sturdy black beauty for nearly forty years, until, one evening when I was out, a clumsy slave knocked over a candelabra and set fire to the lair. I returned to find the air rich with the smell of walnuts, and the Little Lincoln burnt down to a tiny pile of nothing. I felt the same sense of sad disbelief as when I'd heard that Lincoln was dead, and I was none too pleased when I had to pass the following unhappy and uncomfortable day in a beat-up old steamer trunk. I hoped to have old Baboescu build me another, but he had long ago retired to a custom-made coffin of his own.

I've had many coffins since then, but none of them have been worth a thing compared to that one. Here's to Baboescu. The man was an artist.

A coffin is more than a sturdy bed with a door. It's a place for you to shut out the light of day, and temporarily shut down your body. You are likely to have yours for many years, so bear that in mind when selecting one, and let it speak to your personal tastes. Be thoughtful when assessing the advantages of a coffin's sturdy, secured exterior, its unique detailing, or its complementary cushioned, plush interior. If you are careful in your choosing, you will be happy for hundreds of years, enjoying a well-deserved rest in everlasting comfort.

36

TRAVEL

AT SOME POINT, every vampire will find it necessary to travel to another town, state, country, or even continent. The fact that travel is no longer a simple matter of buying a ticket or renting a car is a hard concept for the newly turned vampire to embrace. From here to eternity, every trip that you cannot make by foot is an ordeal.

Long-distance travel is now both inconvenient and unsafe. It exposes you to the risk of sunlight and discovery by humans. Though it may be distasteful, you must think of yourself more as cargo than as a passenger, because you will largely be putting your safe transit into the hands of another. You must prepare with maximum safety in mind.

When you make your arrangements, make sure you allow for one night for every two hundred miles. Leave yourself escape and dormancy options. Keep a reflective Mylar blanket and a body bag with you at all times. It's better to have them and not need them than need them and be without. Finally, bring your scrapbooking kit. Nothing is worse than enduring four days of travel without some means of entertainment.

FLYING

When traveling distances greater than two hundred miles, your first instinct will be to book a late-night flight that arrives at your destination before sunrise. Unfortunately, we live in a world of variables, and nothing exemplifies this more than air travel. Even if your flight takes off on time and touches down without incident, it could sit on the runway for hours until a gate is open.

This leaves you with one place to escape the rising sun: the lavatory. However, it is neither safe nor practical to hide in an airplane lavatory for fourteen hours.

For these reasons, flying is not recommended.

Unless you own a jet, the only way you should fly is as freight. Any funeral director can have a body shipped from one city to another, provided there is a funeral home at the other end willing to pick you up. These arrangements are best handled by a human slave, so that he can track your coffin and make sure you arrive safely and are not lost in transit.* Of course, you are then at the mercy of baggage handlers, who could very easily drop you and expose you to the sunlight, so have your coffin reinforced preflight.

---

*A vampire could easily make the initial phone call, but someone needs to be on hand to play the bereaved relative when the hearse arrives to take the body away. Utilize a discreet funeral service that will not question why they are picking a body up from a private residence and not a morgue.

BOAT

For journeys from Europe to the United States or vice versa, or if you are planning on traveling along the Mississippi or across the Great Lakes, the boat is a feasible manner of transit.

With nautical travel, there are multiple options. You can choose to pack your coffin in a larger freight box and get on a cargo ship to an out-of-the-way locale, or, for oceanic trips to popular destinations, you can board a cruise liner as a passenger. In either case, comfort is assured. A shipping container can be customized into a mini-domicile and stocked with a number of diversions—even a food source—that will keep you entertained for the duration.* On a cruise liner, the cheaper, less-desirable rooms are always the ones away from the outer hull, so your chances of exposure to sunlight are zero, and because of the volume of passengers, no one will notice that you come out only at night.

The duration of the trip will require you to feed from a limited pool of victims several times. If on a cruise, wait until you are in a port, then go ashore at night and feed there. If this is not possible, choose a strong-looking male passenger, drain him completely, and toss him into the ocean. People will assume he was intoxicated and

---

*Do not bring live humans with you for food. They are inconveniently large and have a tendency to bang on the walls when they find themselves imprisoned in dark enclosed spaces. Instead, just bring a cooler stocked with sufficient bags of blood and dry ice.

> **MILES SAYS:**
> I wish my own trek from the Old Country to America could have been made in such comfort. However, at the time there was no such thing as a pleasure cruise or a diesel engine. A transatlantic voyage took seven weeks, on average. My own journey lasted fifty-one days and was spent in a crate labeled "Slovakian Hymnals." I hoped that description would keep thieving hands from prying open the lid. It worked, but the crate was uncomfortable, the waters choppy, and I was always hungry. Just once on that damnable trip, I wanted to drink my fill, but the last thing I needed was to reduce the efficacy of the crew; the men were already suffering from scurvy, which compounded my troubles as it made their blood less vital. My diet of rats and gulls soured me on nautical travel for years. It was only when I was assured of nicer accommodations that I returned to my homeland for a visit.

fell overboard. If you are on a cargo ship, you must feed more judiciously. Only so many sailors can disappear before the crew starts opening crates to find the reason. Instead of draining a victim via his neck, take a bite from the legs of several crewmen. It will require more time, but the resultant lethargy they suffer will be attributed to a flu or a viral outbreak instead of a vampire attack.

TRAIN

Like the airplane, the passenger train is not a reliable means of transit. The whole thing moves slowly, is lined on both sides with large windows, and, depending on where you live, can be completely unreliable. You could get a "sleeper car" and seal it up, but it would take just one errant porter opening your door in daytime to turn the sleeper car into a smoking car. Only when traveling relatively short distances, such as Philadelphia to Washington, D.C., is the passenger train a good alternative.

There are more advantages to the freight train. Many trains will carry shipping containers (like boats), and they can be delivered via tractor-trailer from the train yard to just about anywhere, so you can remain ensconced in door-to-door comfort.

If hiring a freight container and truck is outside of your price range, it is easy, though risky, to hop on a boxcar. The downside is that you will be unable jump aboard with your coffin, so you will have to create your own makeshift lair with a large tarp and duct tape in the far recesses of the car. The upside is that fellow passengers are transients who will not be missed if dispatched.

DRIVING

Though not as fast, the automobile is one of your safest options for long-distance travel. You dictate the schedule, can pull off whenever you need to in order to rest or feed, and can go anywhere the highway does. The best vehicle for this is a cargo van with a tinted windshield. The tinting should be UV-resistant and heavy enough so that if you are caught in a sunrise, you'll have enough time to pull over and climb in back. These coffins on wheels can be so comfortable that some choose to live in them!

TUNNELING

Generally, the tunnel is convenient only for short distances, but as an immortal, you have ample time to construct an elaborate system of tunnels that span as far as you have patience to dig. In urban areas, you can tap into the existing network of sewer, municipal, and possibly subway tunnels to extend your reach, and many border towns have makeshift tunnels stocked with ample prey. Be careful to reinforce your tunnels, though. You don't want to spend your eternity buried fifty feet underground, feeding on whatever bugs crawl into your mouth.

37

IS MENTORING FOR YOU?

OF ALL THE POWERS you have gained, the ability to transform whomever you wish into a vampire is the most profound. However, this is not just another power. It is a gift. The experience is as awe-inspiring and humbling as giving birth. It is an act that can bring seismic changes to every aspect of your existence, and it indelibly links you to another being.

Unfortunately, too many new vampires view this power as a novelty, something to be tossed out like Mardi Gras beads. In reality, bringing even a single vampire into the fold comes with significant responsibility. You have your whole eternal life ahead of you, and it would be a major mistake to rush into the yoke of mentorship so soon.

A vampire who is turned carelessly and not provided with proper nurturing can unwittingly do much harm to himself, and the negative effects can easily ripple through all of vampirekind. For this reason, turning another is discouraged until you are at least one hundred years old and have enough perspective and experience to make the right decisions.

As you initially confront your own immortality, you may also panic about the mortality of your loved ones and feel compelled to "save" them. It may seem harsh, but it is almost always a regrettable decision to turn a human family member. Not everyone sees eternal life as a positive, particularly those with a gross dislike of change. If your human parents still cannot figure out how to use call-waiting, the technological complexities of the coming centuries will mentally drown them. You will likely have a frustrating time getting your siblings to take your tutelage seriously, especially if they still call you by an embarrassing nickname. Plus, every irritating quirk you barely managed to tolerate before will cause a molten core of rage to grow inside you as the centuries pass.

When you are ready to make your first turn, you want a blank slate—a vampire you can grow with, not one who will spend the next thousand years bringing up that incident in the hot dog–stand bathroom when you were twelve. No one checks his baggage at the door of everlasting life.

WHEN THE TIME IS RIGHT

Every vampire was turned for some reason. Think about why you were chosen. Was it your wealth, connections, engineering degree, fluency in Old English? Sadly, it was probably none of these things. Since you are referring to this book, you were in all likelihood turned irresponsibly by someone who had no interest in mentoring. You may only remember an enigmatic guy at a party who liked your shirt or laughed at your joke about four rabbis making a sandwich. Come the next night you were a vampire, and he was gone.

Bringing someone into the fold for temporary companionship can be a grave mistake. A lonely vampire is much better served by joining a coven or seeking out another vampire for short-term relations. When you turn someone just so you can pal around with him, it's easy to make great misjudgments of character. By bestowing the gift of immortality, you are creating an eternal bond. The foundation of an eternal bond is not formed on the mutual appreciation of prog rock or pinball.

MILES SAYS:
I made only one rash, regrettable turning choice in my life. It ended up launching a pretty unpleasant domino effect, and it's the reason most vampires steer clear of Gaithersburg, Maryland.

Your charge should be someone who will fill a current need in your life, whether intellectual or practical, but who also exhibits qualities that could become an asset to the greater vampire community. A vampire feeling particularly unmoored in time might seek out a savvy young human who can guide him through the kaleidoscopic chaos of the era. Others target shipping magnates to accommodate their travels or recently cashed-out entrepreneurs with the means to finance a comfortable new century. On occasion you may encounter a human who doesn't have much to offer you personally but has a personality so suitable for vampire life that it would seem a waste to leave him with the warm. Turn him for the greater good.

Optimally, you should spend at least one hundred years guiding

A mentor should never leave questions unanswered, particularly during important physical changes.

A good mentor encourages his student and celebrates his milestones.

and sharing your experience with your ward. It's a sizable commitment, but it is bound to enrich your eternal life as much as your new vampire's.

Eventually there will come a time when he is ready to leave the lair and take charge of his own immortality. As you help carry his bags and coffin to the curb, do so not with sorrow but with pride. If you've taught him well, he will safely make it through many nights to come and you will see each other again in the future.

Remember, all vampires you create are instilled with the same powers you possess, including the ability to turn their own. One bad turn can easily beget many more, and it's in no one's interest for the community to be overrun by ill-considered and ill-suited vampires. You are transferring a legacy and possibly even creating a dynasty. The simple act of thinking before your fangs take the plunge can have an impact that lasts forever. Choose well.

ANATOMY OF A BAD TURN: MILES'S MISTAKE IN MARYLAND

- Miles meets ne'er-do-well tippler Henry Meadow at a cocktail party and is charmed by the madcap tales he

tells of his society life. Dazzled by his performance, Miles turns Henry, who quickly runs off to try out his new powers before Miles can teach him a thing.
- Unaware that as a vampire he can no longer consume alcohol, Henry immediately turns his layabout brother-in-law, Stephen, solely because he makes a marvelous Manhattan.
- Bored out of his mind now that he can't drink, Henry turns a mediocre children's puppeteer to entertain him.
- Stephen, in turn, uses the gift of immortality to settle up with a loan shark.
- The puppeteer turns the proprietor of the handicrafts shop that stocks his favorite felts and comical buttons.
- The loan shark turns the last honest judge in Gaithersburg so he can no longer preside during normal court hours.
- The proprietor turns her rascally old grandpap and two cousins who dropped out of school and have no other prospects.
- Henry turns another drunk out of spite.

APPENDICES

Appendix 1

THE RULING FAMILIES

THE RULING FAMILIES each represent the interests of a continent and are the oldest known vampire covens. Though they originated in Eastern Europe, when the High Council was formed, it was determined that each continent must have a Ruling Family in residence to arbitrate regional feuds. In an event known as the Ruling Family Diaspora, members journeyed to their respective territories, altered their names, and immersed themselves in their new cultures. For their historical perspective, longevity, and unmatched abilities, they are given the utmost respect.

NORTH AMERICA
The Goodman Family
BASED IN
Santa Cruz, California
HIGH COUNCIL REPRESENTATIVE
The Vampire Satchel Goodman

APPENDICES

SOUTH AMERICA
The Álvarez Family
BASED IN
Buenos Aires, Argentina
HIGH COUNCIL REPRESENTATIVE
The Vampire Lucia Álvarez

ASIA
The Rawat Family
BASED IN
New Delhi, India
HIGH COUNCIL REPRESENTATIVE
The Vampire Jayashree Rawat

ANTARCTICA
The Vampire Rod Fig*
BASED IN
Queen Maud Land, Antarctica
HIGH COUNCIL REPRESENTATIVE
The Vampire Rod Fig

EUROPE
The Lefebvre Family
BASED IN
Lyon, France
HIGH COUNCIL REPRESENTATIVE
The Vampire Maximilien Lefebvre

*The Vampire Rod Fig has yet to be called upon to settle a dispute, but the Ruling Families felt it prudent to install an Antarctic representative in the event that global warming forces future generations of vampires to live on the continent in order to follow their prey.

AFRICA
The Kiprop Family
BASED IN
Eldoret, Kenya
HIGH COUNCIL REPRESENTATIVE
The Vampire Samson Kiprop

AUSTRALIA
The Walker Family
BASED IN
Perth, Australia
HIGH COUNCIL REPRESENTATIVE
The Vampire Hugh Walker

Appendix 11

GLYPH GUIDE

—	Dinner hosts pushy, tough to avoid eating
—	Dark, enclosed place to sleep
—	Quality slave candidate
—	Slave – do not kill
—	Slave – lost mind, OK to kill
—	Beware of skylights
—	Underused shed in backyard
—	Ample prey population
—	Blood-borne diseases reported
—	Alley safe for killing
—	Discount body bag supplier
—	Coven territory – membership closed
—	Coven territory – accepting members
—	Coven territory – referrals only
—	Reliable store for current casual fashions
—	Tube socks sold in bulk
—	High vampire awareness area
—	Low vampire awareness area
—	Safe house
—	Sunrises may advance quickly

APPENDICES

Symbol	Meaning
	Impressionable youths
	 Vampire dental services available
	Merchant has convenient night hours
	 Rare species area – do not feed on animals
	 Under-staffed orphanage
	 House of mirrors
	 Invite-only residence
	 Familiar-rich area
	 Blood bank
	 Romantic treetop
	 Town suffers frequent natural disasters
	 No warm-blooded life-forms for 30 miles
	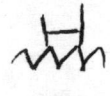 History museum with inaccuracies
	 Solid house band
	 Creepy vampire fanatics
	 Free WiFi hotspot
	 Wildfire danger high
	 Vampire-friendly accountant
	Garlic stench inside
	 Grinning Man spotted
	 Hotel has blackout blinds
	 Slayer zone
	 24-hour gym
	 Bat house certified vampire-free
	 Bat house may contain vampires
	 Van for sale
	 Vampire fiction book club
	 Good tailor
	 Airport with excessive delays
	 This movie sucks

Appendix III

TEMPORARY LAIRS

VACANT BIG BOX STORE

Take note of the number and size of weeds in the parking lot to date how long the building has been vacant.

LAIR-CONVERSION PROCESS:
- Disable any video surveillance systems.
- Gather all mannequins from around the building and crowd them en masse to block the front entryway, arms extended in a greeting when possible.
- Any leftover mannequins can be placed in a line from the front of the store leading to the break-room table.
- Construct a coffin high up on the racking in the shipping and receiving department.
- The door employees once used to go outside and smoke can serve as an entrance and exit.

TWO- OR THREE-STORY UNSOLD MCMANSION HOME

These dwellings are increasingly often compromised by squatters or scavengers. The sound of a window being broken is a bell for you to feed.

LAIR-CONVERSION PROCESS:
- Block exterior doorways on the first floor with granite countertops, stainless steel appliances, and specialized wine storage units.
- Locate the attic access hole.

- Two-by-fours lying around the unfinished basement can be constructed into a rudimentary coffin, which you can then place in the spacious attic.
- Use the decorative gable vent as entrance and exit.

THREE- TO FIVE-STORY CONDEMNED BUILDING

Always keep tabs on the building's future. Demolition notices are typically posted well in advance, but have an alternate safe house established in the area.

LAIR-CONVERSION PROCESS:
- Disable all fire escapes.
- Board up all top-floor windows not already covered with plywood.
- Install your coffin on the top level.
- Pile debris in the stairwell until it is completely blocked.
- If there is an elevator, tear the cable supporting the car until it plunges to the bottom of the shaft. Also, disable any ladder that might be in the shaft.
- Use the roof access as entrance and exit. Scale up and down the building or leap to a nearby rooftop.

Appendix 16
ONLINE RESOURCES

DISCLOSURE STATEMENT: Though I would be promoting all of these Web start-ups regardless of my involvement, my lawyers have informed me that I must notify readers of my majority shareholder stake in all of the companies profiled below. If you want to know why I would invest so much of my personal fortune in these inspired online endeavors, I strongly encourage you to visit the sites, use them frequently, and tell other vampires if you find them effective or enjoyable.

—THE VAMPIRE MILES PROCTOR

In this new age of information sharing, vampires are continuing to unlock the potential of technological innovation, and the following three incredible online resources are leading the way.

THE KARZACK PROJECT: HARNESSING THE DEADLY POWER OF COLLABORATION

When the Vampire Heinrich Karzack was turned in 1997, he thought his two decades of computer programming experience would no longer be of use. All of his nighttime hours were spent adjusting to the new existence. Though he reveled in his new powers, what infuriated Karzack was his sudden incapacity to get into invite-only buildings. After finally seeing the flash of the fang from some friendly vampires and sharing his frustration with them, the Vampire Heinrich learned that the inability to enter certain homes was a problem that had plagued vampires for thousands of years.

Previously, the Vampire Heinrich had seen no way to link his computer expertise with his bloodthirst, but after researching this long-standing problem, he realized how he could make a positive difference. He embarked on a new project that only weeks later culminated in the launch of www.karzack.org.

Nicknamed "Wikillpedia," the Karzack Project is now a revolutionary vampire-only online resource. Using open-source technol-

"I was making so many mistakes at first, and I couldn't get in anywhere! I knew I couldn't be the only vampire with this problem," says the Vampire Heinrich, sitting in the Palo Alto offices of KarzackMedia, Inc.

White House – Karzack Project, The Free Entry Information Database
www.karzack.org
Log in / create account
article
discussion
view source
history
White House
From The Karzack Project
(Redirected from White house)
KARZACK
The Free Entry Information Database
navigation
Main page
Contents
Featured content
Current events
Random article
search
Go
Search
interaction
About Karzack
Community portal
Recent changes
Contact Karzack
Donate to Karzack
Help
toolbox
What links here
Related changes
Upload file
Special pages
Printable version
Permanent link
Cite this page
languages
For other uses, see White House (disambiguation).
See also: Executive Office of the President of the United States
The White House is the official residence and principal workplace of the President of the United States. Located at 1600 Pennsylvania Avenue NW in Washington, D.C., it houses prey type Bs, with the exception of one prey type D, which can only be hunted if his/her approval ratings are exceedingly low.
Contents [hide] [hide]
1 Entryways
1.1 North Portico
1.2 Diplomatic Reception Entrance
1.3 Truman Balcony
1.4 Underground Escape Pod Silo
2 Entry Covers
2.1 After-Hours Tour Groups
2.2 Foreign Envoys/Official State Dinners
2.3 Super Bowl Champions
2.4 Oil Industry Lobbyists
3 Obstacles
3.1 Secret Service Agents
3.2 Rooftop Snipers
3.3 Ambitious Interns
3.4 Chief Usher
3.5 First Family and Pets
4 Getting Press Corps Credentials
5 Inaccuracies in 'The West Wing'
6 Layout Plans
White House
South façade of the White House
Government Building/Private Residence
Suggested Vampire Experience 300+ Years
Town 1600 Pennsylvania Avenue NW Washington, D.C. 20500
Country United States
Construction
Started October 13, 1792
Design team
Architect James Hoban

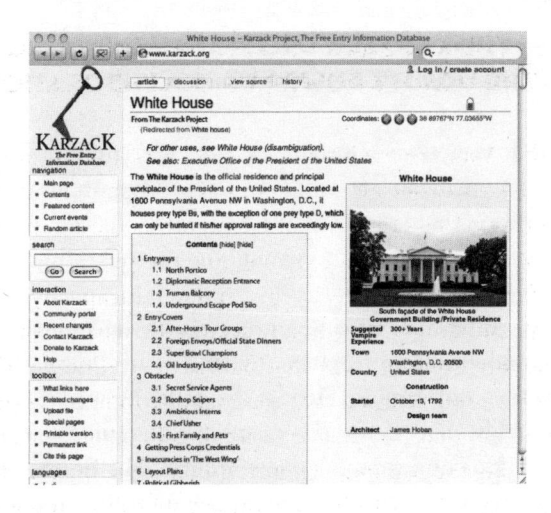

ogy, users can log on from anywhere in the world and enter information about how to get an invitation into virtually any type of building. Thousands of new entries appear daily, and the pages can be updated quickly as a location's invitation requirements change. This is a vast improvement over early, inadequate handbooks such as 1785's *Vognalia's Abode Entry Guide,* which were out-of-date a month after publication.

From caves in Waziristan to penthouses in Monaco, vampires everywhere can learn from their peers about how to get into places once thought impenetrable, and thanks to KarzackMedia's commitment to innovation, vampires can now use the Karzack4Mobile application to get the information on their smartphones, even while standing in an entryway.

> "It feels great to be able to help so many vampires, but it's becoming so popular that bandwidth is getting expensive. That's why I can't thank the Vampire Miles Proctor enough for his generous financial support of the site. He's a credit to us all."
>
> —THE VAMPIRE HEINRICH KARZACK

FIRSTVAMPLIFE: LETTING VAMPIRES RELIVE THEIR BYGONE LIVES

"The Internet has always been a place where individuals can pretend to be whoever they want to be. Why shouldn't that go for vampires too?"

—THE VAMPIRE SIGMUND BROVALDO

Being immortal means making sacrifices. For the Vampire Sigmund Brovaldo, making a sacrifice meant giving up his beloved identity as an Oklahoma dirt farmer during the Dust Bowl era. The years passed quickly, and soon the Vampire Sigmund was the only being—living or undead—for miles around. His neighbors had either moved to the cities to find work, gone off to war, died of starvation, or met their end by the vampire's fangs. "I got lonely," says Brovaldo, who now lives in Boston.

Eventually, the isolated vampire moved on, living out new lives in Japan, Denmark, and Bolivia before returning to the States in 2005. Despite the passage of time, however, Brovaldo could never shake his fondness for the rustic serenity of Depression-era Oklahoma. Ironically, technology would be the key to reliving his tech-free past.

A screen-shot from an 1860s-themed online world on FirstVampLife.com

Like many vampires, the Vampire Sigmund frequently created false identities in online chat rooms in order to lure victims. He posed as everything from a nerdcore hip-hop fan to an expert wood turner, but one night while feeling nostalgic, he pretended to be his old dirt-farmer self. That's when the idea hit him to build an online application where vampires could be who they once were.

Enter FirstVampLife.com, where registered "Vusers" can rebuild the landscapes of their favorite former lives and relive their favorite identities. The online virtual world even allows Vusers to jump into any FirstVampLife scenario and interact with like-minded vampires.

The first scenario Brovaldo designed was a replica of his old Oklahoma town, complete with a general store, a barren cabbage field, and dead Okies who never made it to California. He sent the link to a few friends, they signed on, and for the first time in seventy years, the restless vampire felt like he was back home. Soon more vampires logged on, and now the site features everything from Wild West worlds to scenarios as specific as a Chinese Boxer Rebellion world.

FirstVampLife does have its critics. Some in the community believe it's not healthy for vampires to sit in front of a computer all night long pretending to be somebody they once were, but the Vampire Sigmund pays little attention to those naysayers. "What's the big deal?" he says. "There's nothing wrong with a little escapism. Besides, we're immortal. It's not like we're wasting our lives."

FANGFAIL.COM: A SIMPLE SOUND EFFECT FOR THOSE TIMES WHEN YOU MISS

Not all vampire websites are about utility or connecting with your past. Some are there just to entertain and distract you while you're stuck in the lair. Capitalizing on a phrase his coven members would use to rib each other whenever they missed a vein, the Vampire Deacon McShane set up a simple site that is now one of the most visited vampire destinations on the Web.

"One time my mate got a chunk of down vest stuck on his fangs,"

Fang Fail
www.FangFail.com
Fang Fail!
SHARE
Find Easy Prey In Your Area
Thousands of veins just waiting to be pierced!
www.VampMealFinder.com
Brain Hemorrhage Inducing Ringtones
Kill mortals without extending a fang. The dancing otter ringtone that swept the European vampire community!
www.SanguineSong.com
Work From Inside Your Coffin
It's easy! Learn the secrets that even High Council members don't know about!
www.blood4all.com

the freewheeling, shaggy-haired two-hundred-something says from high atop his Nepalese summer home. The sight of his friend's feather-stuffed mouth caused the whole coven to spontaneously shout, "Fang fail!" And just like that, a hit website was born. Does it do anything besides play a clip of the Vampire McShane's coven shouting the eponymous phrase? No. But that just might be the genius of it.

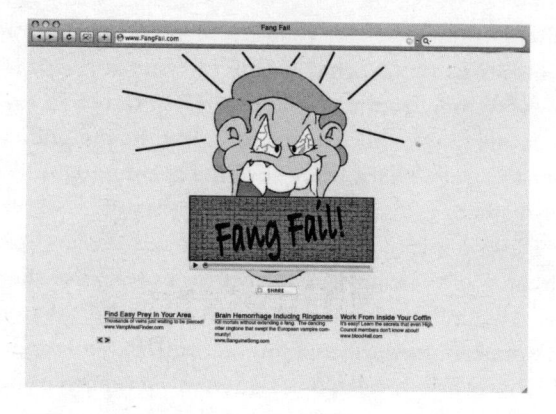

Glossary

ALLUSION An expression designed to subtly reveal vampiric identity.
ANIMALTARIANISM The practice of drinking the blood of animals instead of drinking the blood of humans.
BIT BAG A device that is used to covertly stash food in social situations with humans.
BITE DIFFICULTY The amount of jaw strength required to hold down struggling prey, measured in pounds per square inch.
BLOOD SWEATS A state caused by overfeeding where blood weeps uncontrollably through the skin.
CORNER DWELLER A strain of *Prey Type A*, often found at social gatherings to which he was accidentally invited.
COVENS Small social units of vampires bound by common aesthetics, purposes, and goals.
CULLING GROUNDS Areas where high concentrations of potential human prey gather.
EROTIC AHEMOPHYXIA A psychosexual condition in which a vampire is aroused by resisting the scent of blood.

FAMILIAR A demon spirit housed in the body of an animal that can be engaged to perform a number of specialized services for vampires.

FANG-CARE KIT A customized collection of tools to keep fangs and other teeth in peak condition.

GENERAL-ACCESS AREAS Buildings and locations where vampires need no invitation to enter.

HEMO-DENSE PHEROMONES Chemical byproducts of high-vitality blood that are expressed through the mouth and synthesized during the hemo-libidinal exchange.

HEMO-LIBIDINAL EXCHANGE The neurobiological process by which vampires are sexually attracted to each other.

HEMO-PHOTON PARTICLES Sub-atomic particles released as a by-product of converting blood to energy.

HIGH COUNCIL A group of esteemed vampires that convenes to pass down judgments in personal grievance matters pertaining to the entire vampire community.

HIGH-VITALITY BLOOD Blood that is prized for its potency and superior nutritive qualities.

HYBRID STRUCTURES Buildings and locations where vampires need an invitation to access some, but not all, parts of the structure.

HYPERDRACULA COGNITION A phenomenon in which the mortal public becomes acutely aware of vampire activities, often as a result of a high-profile killing.

IMPRESSIVE-AUTOMOBILE EXTRACTION METHOD A popular method used during the isolation phase of luring that utilizes a stylish motor vehicle in order to entice prey.

INVERSE HIERARCHICAL SUBLIMATION An intra-coven social state in which an older vampire with a youthful appearance must temporarily relinquish his authority to a younger vampire with an older appearance while in public.

INVITE-ONLY BUILDING A location where vampires need an explicit invitation in order to enter the premises.

KILLS See *Prey Type A*.

KREISLANDER METHOD A steady, controlled, effective method of puncturing the neck in order to bleed a victim.

LAIR WATCHMAN A human slave who protects a vampire's lair from intruders.

LURING Regulatory process used to screen prey types to determine their fitness for consumption; divided into selection, seduction, and isolation phases.

MICROBURSTS Rapid actions that require a great deal of energy.

MIND CONTROL The ability to remotely control a human's thoughts and actions.

NIGHT FOOT Colloquial term for a fungal infection of the foot caused by the vampire's natural waste removal process and infrequent sock-changing.

OLD SOUL SYNDROME A feeling of disconnect with the current cultural values and norms of humans under the age of thirty, often experienced by vampires who appear youthful.

OVERFEEDING Consuming blood past the point of satiety.

PERMANENT FANGS The primary set of fangs that elongate before feeding.

PERMANENT VAMPIRE TEETH The complete set of vampire bone teeth, which include fangs, pin teeth, and social teeth.

PIN TEETH Two sets of narrow teeth that reside behind the upper and lower front teeth. During the act of killing, they elongate to assist in optimal blood extraction.

POWER X A power that is different for every vampire and is attained at or around the thousand-year mark; can range from predicting the future or changing one's features to being able to administer static shocks at will.

PREY TYPE A The most abundant type of prey, commonly known as "kills," whose disappearance will go largely unnoticed.

PREY TYPE B Prey who make important contributions to society in the fields of science, the arts, politics, and philanthropy; most people will not notice their absence.

PREY TYPE C Prey that is generally unsafe to kill due to their ability to cause a national news story based on their good looks.

PREY TYPE D Prey that should not be killed due to extreme notability.

PURIFIED BLOOD Human blood that has been consumed and had impurities removed via the liver.

SANGUINARIAN A strange and disturbing human who drinks blood.

SCRAPBOOKING Cutting and pasting memories into art.

SLAVE A human who aligns himself with a vampire to attend to the vampire's daily needs.

SOCIAL TEETH Teeth that are no longer useful to vampires but that are still replicated in vampire bone for human social interaction.

THE VAMPIRE The formal, gender-neutral title for vampires.

THREE PARENTS The entities needed to create a new vampire and pass on their genetic code; made up of the human mother, the human father, and the master vampire.

VAMPIRE "BABY FANGS" The non-elongating fangs that sprout from the human cuspids within an hour of turning.

VAMPIRE FANATICS Mortals who are obsessed with vampires as they have come to understand them through inaccurate pop-culture portrayals.

VAMPIRE GLYPHS Symbols that vampires leave for one another to covertly communicate in public places.

VAMPIRE TIME A base-120 time system that is better suited to the realities of vampire life than the human base-60 time system.

VAMPIRO-NORMATIVE CONSTRUCTS Traditional, often conservative, views of vampirosexuality that often reject vampire-human relationships.

VAMPIROSEXUAL Involving or characterized by sexual attraction between vampires.

VESTIGIAL EMOTIONS Feelings toward humans, often sentimental in nature, from a vampire's previous mortal existence that are still present despite their lack of function.

Afterword

DO YOU FEEL IT NOW, the wondrous power of your new vampiric self? If so, it is time for you to share what you have learned with other new vampires by purchasing a copy of *The New Vampire's Handbook: A Guide for the Recently Turned Creature of the Night* for them. Borrowing books may lead to feuds, so it is best that everyone have their own copy. Finally, now that you have mastered all that is in this tome, keep your eyes out for future installments of my *Vampire's Handbook* series. What you have read is only a taste of what is to come . . .

I REMAIN ETERNALLY YOURS,
THE VAMPIRE MILES PROCTOR

Acknowledgments

ACTION 5 WOULD LIKE to thank those friends and family members we have mentioned in previous tomes, in addition to the following: Robert Austin; Jeremy Barr; Karl Biewald; Bono; Jane Burns; the Camacho family; Shannon Casey; Thayer Christodoulo; Dan Coca; Baly Cooley; Anthony D'Ambrosi; Joisan Decker; Ryan Doherty; Coert Voorhees Henke Donohue; Michelle Faisca; Nelson Faisca; Nuno Faisca; Elizabeth Fisher; Emily Flake; Zach Frechette; Alan Gallo; Caroline Gallo; Christine Gallo; Giulia Gallo; Kathy Gallo; Marie Gallo; Mary Gallo; Remy Gallo; Richard Gallo; Camille Rose Garcia; Barbara, Harold, and Matthew Ginsburg; Ethan Goldman; Daniel Greenberg; Dan Guterman; Todd Hanson; John Harris; Brandon Haynes; Chris Henkel; Ed Herbstman; Morgan Hersch; Arty Holdman; Brendan Holdman; Brian Holdman; Erica Holdman; Karen Holdman; Kevin Holdman; John Huston and Huston Design; Jenny Jackson; Kirsten Johnson; Chris Karwowski; Dave Kornfeld; Christopher James Kramer; David Kurs; Josephine Lacertosa; Saverio Lacertosa; Jonathan Lam; Joe Lerman; Rebecca Licht; Mike Loew; Joan McDonald; Thomas Earl McGraw; Sam Means; Doug Moe; Jeffrey

Morfit; Matt Morrison; Ross Mudrick; Josephine Napolitano; Sarah-Doe Osborne; Michael Ostrow; Randy Ostrow; Teddy Ostrow; Amber Perkins; Rob Pesce; Katherine Pfau; Drew Pisarra; Amanda Power; Joe Randazzo; Jared Ranere; Bettie Rinehart; Mille Ripa; Jay Ross; Heather Sabin; Erica Sackin; Lauren Sarver; Lucille Schrippa; Dan Schwerin; Glen Severance; Nina Sharma; Kelly Shea; JJ Shebesta; Leigh and Beryl Sherman; Joanna Shields; Victoria Skurnick; Smartie; Emma Spear Brodsky; Debra Spector; Morgan Spurlock; Scott Stapleton; Nick Stefanovich; Josh Stein; Emma Trank; Joshua Trank; Rozina Vavetsi; The Village Bar; and, as usual, Mum and Pops Serwacki for the booze and Terry Rose for the guns.

And a very special thanks to Bruce Tracy.

ABOUT THE AUTHORS

Action 5 is a comedy-writing collective based in New York and Wisconsin. The group's two previous books, *The Dangerous Book for Dogs* and *The Devious Book for Cats,* are available from Villard. For more information about these books and other random projects, please visit www.action5.com.

Individually, Action 5's members are:

JOE GARDEN was born above a bar in Chicago and has lived up to that high standard ever since. He is currently the features editor of *The Onion*. In addition, he has appeared in two films (one straight to DVD, one unreleased), a bizarre and unusual cartoon, and has, with his wife, Anita, written two episodes of the Emmy Award–winning educational cartoon *Word Girl*. Joe lives in Brooklyn with said wife and three cats.

JANET GINSBURG is a Brooklyn-based writer and producer whose work has appeared on *The Daily Show with Jon Stewart* on Comedy Central, as well as the Discovery, Sci-Fi, and E! Entertainment television networks. A former staff writer for *The Onion,* she has to date watched more than eight hundred episodes of ABC's 1966–71 daytime gothic soap opera, *Dark Shadows*. It's quite a commitment.

ABOUT THE AUTHORS

CHRIS PAULS lives in Middleton, Wisconsin, where he pumps out strings of words that sometimes earn him money. He is a contributing writer for *The Onion* and plays guitar as time permits.

ANITA SERWACKI is a contributing writer for *The Onion* and has written for the PBS animated series *Word Girl*. She served as music supervisor for the documentary *The Kid Stays in the Picture* and has been a DJ for many years, most notably on the New York City burlesque circuit. As previously noted by husband Joe Garden, she lives in Brooklyn with him and three cats.

SCOTT SHERMAN is a staff writer for *Important Things with Demetri Martin* on Comedy Central. He is a former contributing writer for *The Onion* and *The Onion News Network,* and has also written for *The New York Times Magazine* and several enjoyable television channels. He lives in New York City.

ABOUT THE ILLUSTRATORS

CAROLITA JOHNSON was conceived in Manhattan, grew up in Queens, and came of age in Paris, France, where she modeled her way through many a tiny garret and pursued studies in medieval anthropology. In spite of the lure of a dusty existence in the manuscript room of the French national library, Carolita returned to New York to fall back on cartooning and became a regular contributor to *The New Yorker*. She is (surprise, surprise) working on her own book, which you will no doubt hear about soon enough.

SHANNON WHEELER, a contributor to *The New Yorker,* an opera writer, and an Eisner Award–winning cartoonist, is best known for his creation *Too Much Coffee Man*. His previous books include *Too Much Coffee Man's Amusing Musings, Parade of Tirade, Guide for the Perplexed,* and *How to Be Happy.* He lives in Portland, Oregon, with his kids. He rarely sleeps.

ABOUT THE PHOTOGRAPHERS

MICHAEL FAISCA grew up in Portugal but was born in New York City, where he decided to return after earning his BA in graphic design. He worked as a photo editor on the bestselling book *Our Dumb World: Atlas of the Planet Earth* and is now a graphics editor at *The Onion*.

NICK GALLO is a native New Yorker, residing in Brooklyn. He has worked as a photo editor on the book *Our Dumb World: Atlas of the Planet Earth* and as an associate producer on *Big Fan*, a feature-length independent film. Currently, he is a graphics editor at *The Onion*.

ABOUT THE TYPE

This book was set in Fairfield, the first typeface from the hand of the distinguished American artist and engraver Rudolph Ruzicka (1883–1978). In its structure Fairfield displays the sober and sane qualities of the master craftsman whose talent has long been dedicated to clarity. It is this trait that accounts for the trim grace and vigor, the spirited design and sensitive balance, of this original typeface.

Rudolph Ruzicka was born in Bohemia and came to America in 1894. He set up his own shop, devoted to wood engraving and printing, in New York in 1913 after a varied career working as a wood engraver, in photoengraving and banknote printing plants, and as an art director and freelance artist. He designed and illustrated many books, and was the creator of a considerable list of individual prints—wood engravings, line engravings on copper, and aquatints.